FOREIGN INVESTMENTS IN ASIA
A Survey of Problems and Prospects in the 1970s

A. Kapoor

WITH THE ASSISTANCE OF JAMES E. COTTEN

THE DARWIN PRESS
PRINCETON, NEW JERSEY

Library of Congress Catalog Card Number: 79-177976

Second Printing, 1973

ISBN 0-87850-010-3

Printed in the United States of America

Dedicated to James J. Raper,

entrepreneur and multinationalist

FOREIGN INVESTMENTS IN ASIA

CONTENTS

v

TABLES AND GRAPHS

                *   *   *   *   *

The following graphs are included in Chapter 9: "American
Business and the China Market"

FOREWORD

Politically, economically, culturally--and inexorably--the twain are meeting! In this day and age the old "East is East and West is West" adage has been proven as false as the green cheese theory of the moon's structure.

For example, it was the economic miracle of Japan in the East which touched off the international monetary crisis that shook the financial capitals of the West. Similarly, the recent summit meeting of the leaders of China and the U.S.A. in Peking has dramatically altered political and economic postures throughout the world, the full effects of which are still to be felt. While the nation states of Asia display a great diversity of social, religious, and cultural patterns, they share one objective in common--improvement in the living standards of their large, and for the most part rapidly growing, populations through planned economic development. Asia today offers what Professor Kapoor describes as a "new investment frontier" for the American businessman. American investment, although increasing rapidly in certain Asian countries, is still minuscule compared to U.S. investments in Europe and Latin America.

There has not yet developed a "Yankee go home" psychosis to the same extent encountered in Latin America and Europe. Nevertheless, Asian political leaders and businessmen, their sensitivities sharpened by a history of colonial domination, are acutely aware that foreign investments must be regulated in order to serve their country's best interests.

The Japanese have been the first to recognize the business opportunities offered in the lesser developed countries of Asia, and they have moved aggressively to seize these attractive markets. Combining the resources of their manufacturers, banks, trading companies--and with the strong support of their government--the Japanese have mounted an export effort that is the envy of American competitors forced to comply with U.S. anti-trust legislation. Having established strong, if not dominant, market positions there is evidence that Japanese trade is being followed by Japanese investments. The Japanese, being Asian themselves, have an inherent advantage over Americans in understanding how to do business in Asia. It is in this area of understanding Asian thinking and business practices that Professor Kapoor's study, "Foreign Investments in Asia," will be of considerable value to American businessmen interested in the Eastern hemisphere.

Professor Kapoor has drawn extensively on the knowledge and experience of Asian and foreign businessmen now doing business in eight important markets of Northeast, Southeast, and South Asia. He has also interviewed many of the government officials responsible for shaping and administering the economic policies of these countries, correlating their professional and political backgrounds with their attitudes toward foreign investments. On this basis, the authors have projected changes that can be expected as a new generation of leaders take charge in Asia.

The section devoted to the People's Republic of China is particularly timely in light of recent indications that trade relations with the U.S.A. may develop more rapidly than thought possible as late as mid-1972.

Professor Kapoor's knowledge of Asian affairs and his penetrating insight as to Eastern thinking offer invaluable guidelines for newcomers

as well as "old Asian hands" who hope to compete successfully in the complex and structured business environment of Asia.

J. R. Galloway

September, 1972

PREFACE

American companies are showing a dramatic increase of interest in
the Asian region as a result of Asia's large population, impressive
economic gains, political stability, and the search for new investment frontiers. Recently, American companies have also begun to
show a strong interest in the potentially large markets of the
People's Republic of China.

International trade and investment, and in particular that of
the multinational enterprise, which at present is largely an American phenomenon, have grown tremendously in the 1960s. In addition,
the past decade has witnessed a growing conflict between the nation
state and the multinational enterprise, which has been particularly
intense in Latin America. It is not unlikely that a similar conflict
might develop in Asia. At present, however, Asia has received only
a nominal amount of American foreign direct investment, and unlike
Latin America, the conflicts are beginning to emerge before the fact
of foreign investment. An understanding of the motivations of the
investing company and the host country (particularly the host government as the locus of power and the prime agent of change) will contribute to a better understanding between the participating groups and
may result in a reduction of conflict.

The study on the Asian investment climate offers a comparative
picture from the standpoint of foreign investment in eight Asian

countries in Northeast Asia (Japan, South Korea, Taiwan), Southeast Asia (the Philippines, Thailand, Indonesia, Malaysia), and South Asia (India). Corporate executives with responsibilities for one country or subregion can gain information on other countries and compare their views and comments with those of 94 other executives of American companies. Singapore and Hong Kong are not included because of their unique features, which are not representative of the larger Asian region.

The study on trade with the People's Republic of China presents the views of 95 executives of American companies. Because most American companies are still considering what should be their policy and program of action toward the markets of the People's Republic of China, the views of responding companies should prove to be most timely.

The decision-making process of foreign investors and host governments is largely based on subjective expectations. The study on the Asian investment climate endeavors to present the expectations of executives of American companies in terms of what they plan to do and what they expect the policies and practices of host governments in Asia to be. Similarly, the study on "American Business and the China Market" presents the expectations of American companies regarding the problems and prospects of trade with the People's Republic of China.

Detailed tables have been eliminated; instead, graphs are used to present the essential features of the responses.

The study on the Asian investment climate was developed by Ashok Kapoor with the assistance of James E. Cotten, while the study on trade with the People's Republic of China was developed by Professor Kapoor with the assistance of Richard Schmitt.

Appreciation is expressed to the many executives who assisted in the formulation and development of these studies and to those who answered the somewhat complex and time-consuming questionnaires. Understandably, these executives must remain unnamed. Additionally, the painstaking computation and rechecking of figures by Peter Sugges and the assistance in computational work provided by William Toy and Ivar Hegsted is gratefully acknowledged.

J. Roy Galloway has been a constant source of encouragement, and a special note of thanks is due to him.

A. Kapoor
James E. Cotten

September, 1972
New York City

Introduction

An Overview of the Asian Investment Climate

An international enterprise can offer technology, foreign exchange, organization, access to international markets, and other resources which are sought by countries in their efforts to industrialize. While there are areas of agreement and disagreement between the foreign investor and the host governments of developing countries, the agreement is largely in terms of the overall need for resources. The disagreement is largely in terms of the extent of the need, the specific terms and conditions of investment, and the overall mood which characterizes a country's reaction toward a foreign investor. This study presents the subjective expectations of corporate executives of U.S. companies with reference to the general and specific features comprising the foreign investment climate in Asia at present and in five years.

This chapter highlights the characteristics of the investment climates prevalent in the Asian region and in specific Asian countries. More specifically, it deals with the extent of private investments in Asia, the career background of Asian government leaders, the extent and significance of the emerging Asian generation, and the extent and impact of Japanese investments in Asia. An understanding of these features will assist in interpreting the analysis of the responses to the questionnaire.

BROADER ENVIRONMENTAL AND ECONOMIC CONTEXT

Economic Context.* Asia represents about 12% of the world's GNP
(only 7% if Japan is excluded), with Australasia (Australia and New
Zealand) representing an additional 2%. These figures do not reveal
the significance of Asia in the wider world community. Demographic
considerations, however, do give Asia a very different level of importance. Asia, excluding Japan, represents 23% of the world's
population; 31% including Japan; 31.4% including Australasia; and
51.4% including the People's Republic of China. The fact that India's
population of 550 million people roughly equals that of the combined
populations of Latin America and Africa lends additional significance
to these statistics.

In economic terms Asia is relatively poor. Asia--Japan excluded--
has an average annual per capita income of $120 as compared with
Japan's $901, Australasia's $1,600, Europe's $1,590, and North Amer-
ica's $3,476.

AMERICAN INVESTMENTS

The extent of American private investment in Asia is limited. Table 1
shows that U.S. investment in Asia (i.e., Far East in the table) as
of 1969 was $3,363 million or 4.75% of the total U.S. private foreign
investment. In comparison, U.S. investments in other Third World
regions as of 1969 were: Latin America, $11,667 million (16.49%);
Africa, $2,970 million (4.20%); and the Middle East, $1,829 million
(2.58%).

---

*See Appendix A for information on "Indicators of Market Size--Asia."

TABLE 1

U.S. PRIVATE INVESTMENTS[1] IN THE THIRD WORLD
(in millions of dollars)

		1955	1956	1957	1958	1959	1960	1961	1962
Latin America	$	6,233	7,059	7,434	7,751	8,120	8,387	8,236	8,424
	%	32.27	31.83	29.27	28.30	27.22	25.59	23.76	22.63
Africa	$	572	659	664	746	833	925	1,064	1,271
	%	2.96	2.97	2.61	2.72	2.79	2.82	3.07	3.41
Middle East	$	1,027	1,106	1,138	1,224	1,213	1,139	1,240	1,200
	%	5.32	4.99	4.48	4.47	4.07	3.37	3.58	3.22
Far East[2]	$	668	788	881	954	1,024	1,152	1,239	1,300
	%	3.46	3.55	3.47	3.48	3.43	3.51	3.57	3.49

		1963	1964	1965	1966	1967	1968	1969
Latin America	$	8,662	8,894	9,391	9,826	10,265	11,033	11,667
	%	21.29	20.04	19.04	17.96	17.26	16.98	16.49
Africa	$	1,426	1,685	1,918	2,074	2,273	2,674	2,970
	%	3.50	3.80	3.89	3.79	3.83	4.11	4.20
Middle East	$	1,277	1,332	1,536	1,669	1,749	1,805	1,829
	%	3.14	3.00	3.11	3.05	2.94	2.78	2.58
Far East[2]	$	1,515	1,700	2,033	2,227	2,540	2,919	3,363
	%	3.72	4.01	4.12	4.07	4.27	4.49	4.75

[1]Investment refers to book value and does not include portfolio investment.

[2]Far East includes all the countries from Pakistan in the West to Japan in the East; it excludes Mainland China and Australasia.

Source: *Survey of Current Business*, U.S. Department of Commerce. Investment figures are from issues of the *Survey* between 1956 and 1970.

Table 1 shows that the Latin American region has suffered the most dramatic decline in terms of percentage of U.S. investments: from 32.27% in 1955 to 16.49% in 1969. During the same period, the Middle East shows a decline from 5.32% to 2.58%. Asia and Africa are the only Third World regions reflecting a growth. Thus, U.S. investments in Asia as a percent of total U.S. foreign investments increased from 3.46% in 1955 to 4.75% in 1969 while Africa's grew from 2.96% to 4.20%.

An important feature of U.S. private investments in Asia is revealed in Table 2. U.S. private investment in Asia increased largely in Japan, growing from .77% ($254 million) in 1960 to 1.72% ($1,218 million) in 1969. It is important to note that U.S. private investment in the developing countries of Asia increased marginally, ranging from 2.74% ($898 million) in 1960 to 3.039% ($2,145 million) in 1969. In absolute terms, between 1960 and 1969, U.S. private investments in Japan increased by $964 million and for the rest of Asia by $1,247 million.

Table 3 shows U.S. investments in Japan as a percent of total U.S. investments in Asia. Thus, investments increased from 22.05% of total U.S. investments in Asia in 1960 to 36.22% in 1969. (U.S. investment is much larger if portfolio investments are added to the direct investment figure.) As discussed in subsequent chapters, the advantages of the Japanese market (large size, high per capita income, political stability) will continue to draw a growing amount of U.S. private investment, especially as the Japanese liberalize the terms and conditions of private foreign investments.

TABLE 2

U.S. INVESTMENTS IN ASIA
(in millions of dollars)

		1960	1961	1962	1963	1964
Total U.S. Investment World-wide	$	32,778	34,667	37,226	40,686	44,386
Total U.S. Investment Far East	$ %	1,152 3.51	1,237 3.57	1,300 3.49	1,515 3.72	1,780 4.01
Total U.S. Investment Japan	$ %	254 0.77	302 0.87	373 1.00	472 1.16	598 1.35
Total U.S. Investment Far East except Japan	$ %	898 2.74	935 2.70	927 2.49	1,043 2.56	1,182 2.66

		1965	1966	1967	1968	1969
Total U.S. Investment World-wide	$	49,328	54,711	59,486	64,983	70,763
Total U.S. Investment Far East	$ %	2,033 4.12	2,227 4.07	2,540 4.27	2,919 4.49	3,363 4.75
Total U.S. Investment Japan	$ %	675 1.37	756 1.38	870 1.46	1,050 1.62	1,218 1.72
Total U.S. Investment Far East except Japan	$ %	1,358 2.75	1,481 2.69	1,670 2.81	1,869 2.88	2,145 3.03

Source: Same as Table 1.

5

TABLE 3

U.S. INVESTMENT IN JAPAN AS PERCENTAGE
OF TOTAL U.S. INVESTMENT IN ASIA
(in millions of dollars)

	1960	1961	1962	1963	1964
Total Investment in Asia	$1,152	$1,237	$1,300	$1,515	$1,780
Investment in Japan	$ 254	$ 302	$ 373	$ 472	$ 598
Per cent Investment in Japan	22.05%	24.47%	28.69%	31.16%	33.60%

	1965	1966	1967	1968	1969
Total Investment in Asia	$2,033	$2,227	$2,540	$2,919	$3,363
Investment in Japan	$ 675	$ 756	$ 870	$1,050	$1,218
Per cent Investment in Japan	33.20%	33.95%	34.25%	35.97%	36.22%

Source: Same as Table 1.

TABLE 4

DISTRIBUTION OF U.S. INVESTMENTS IN ASIA
(in millions of dollars)

		Mining & Smelting	Petroleum	Manufac- turing	Public Utilities	Trade	Other	Total
1969	$	53	1,303	1,299	41	383	232	3,362
	%	1.58	38.75	38.63	2.71	11.39	6.40	100
1968	$	44	1,158	1,081	81	338	217	2,919
	%	1.51	39.67	37.03	2.77	11.58	7.43	100
1967	$	40	992	924	69	303	208	2,540
	%	1.57	39.06	36.57	2.72	11.93	8.19	100
1966	$	37	913	745	74	271	188	2,227
	%	1.66	41.00	33.45	3.32	12.17	8.44	100
1965	$	34	904	631	58	241	165	2,033
	%	1.67	44.47	31.04	2.85	11.85	8.12	100
1964	$	31	814	517	51	214	152	1,780
	%	1.74	45.73	29.04	2.87	12.02	8.54	100
1963	$	30	714	396	36	189	150	1,515
	%	1.98	47.13	26.14	2.38	12.48	9.90	100
1962	$	29	612	317	36	159	136	1,269
	%	2.29	48.23	24.98	2.84	12.53	10.12	100
1961	$	27	558	293	111	144	109	1,241
	%	2.18	44.96	23.61	8.94	11.60	8.78	100
1960	$	24	536	259	99	130	103	1,152
	%	2.08	46.53	22.48	8.59	11.28	8.94	100

Source: Same as Table 1.

7

Table 4 offers more detailed information on the industry-wise distribution of U.S. investments in Asia between 1960 and 1969. Petroleum shows a decline from 46.53% of total investments in 1960 to 38.75% in 1969; in absolute terms, during the same period petroleum investments increased from $536 million to $1,303 million. Investments in manufacturing reflect a substantial increase, growing from 22.48% ($259 million) in 1960 to 38.63% ($1,299 million) in 1969. Investments in mining and smelting and public utilities have decreased in percentage while they have grown slightly in trade.

U.S. investments in Asia have not been as extensive as elsewhere for several reasons. First, investment opportunities in Western Europe, Canada, and Latin America have had higher priority because of the relative ease of entry, greater knowledge of markets, and a generally favorable reaction (at least in the past) to foreign investors by many host governments. Second, U.S. companies have only recently turned to Asia, especially the developing countries, for investments. One of the reasons is that the political uncertainties which characterize countries achieving independence and consolidating a nation-state have discouraged private foreign investments. Third, host governments have often been ambivalent toward private foreign investors as a result of their preoccupation with what are deemed to be more pressing problems and a fear of foreign capital arising from their experiences under colonialism.

CAREER BACKGROUND OF ASIAN LEADERS

Asian governments play a major role in the economic and business affairs of their countries. The success of a company operating in Asia is

TABLE 5

CAREER BACKGROUNDS OF CURRENT ASIAN LEADERS IN SEVEN COUNTRIES
(work experience before attaining ministerial rank)

Type of Work Experience	1 Politics		2 Secretariat		3 Administration		4 Law/Judiciary		5 Educator/Journalist		6 Social Work		7 Military Police		8 Business		9 Man years in Government
	%	No.	%	No.	%	No.	%	No.	%	No.	%	No.	%	No.	%	No.	
India	78	279	11	38	50	177	29	103	19	68	3	9	–	–	–	–	356
Japan	9	206	9	102	53	138	5	12	18	47	–	–	2	5	30	79	260
S. Korea	16	21	10	13	42	57	7	9	18	25	4	5	36	48	7	9	135
Malaysia	92	164	32	57	49	87	21	37	16	27	5	9	10	18	5	9	178
Pakistan	46	37	19	15	65	52	34	27	15	12	7	6	24	19	7	6	80
Philippines	59	89	20	30	27	41	47	72	32	48	6	9	10	15	32	49	152
Singapore	81	48	15	9	14	8	17	10	42	25	–	–	–	–	17	10	59
Total	69%	844	22%	264	46%	560	22%	270	21%	254	3%	38	9%	105	13%	162	1,220

Compiled by John Shankland and A. Kapoor

1 Was elected to office.
2 Worked in government at a level lower than deputy minister, e.g., section or bureau chief.
3 Appointed as deputy minister or higher.
4 Practicing lawyer or judge.
5 Held a teaching or administrative position in an institution of learning or served as editor of a publication.
6 Worked in a non-profit social agency.
7 Served in armed forces or in police.
8 Worked as a manager or entrepreneur in a profit-oriented, private business.
9 Man year: one individual X one year in office.

9

largely determined by its ability to maintain good relationships with the host government. To deal effectively with Asian governments, however, the foreign investor must be aware of the background of the Asian leaders. Such knowledge is of singular importance because the answers given by the executives in this study are dependent on the policies and programs of action they expect host government officials in Asia to pursue.

Table 5 shows that a very limited number of decision makers in Asian governments have a background in business: only 162 man years (13%) out of a total of 1,200 man years. However, the percentage with a business background varies considerably by country: India, 0%; Malaysia, 5%; South Korea, 7%; Pakistan, 7%; Singapore, 17%; Japan, 30%; and the Philippines, 32%. The experience of decision makers has been in other areas, such as politics, the armed services, civil administration, foreign affairs, and so forth, and such difference leads to serious problems of communication between investors and host governments.

It is noteworthy that 69% of Asian leaders have a background in politics. Even here, there are major variations between countries: Malaysia, 92%; Singapore, 81%; India, 78%; the Philippines, 59%; Pakistan, 46%; South Korea, 16%; Japan, 9%.

Other backgrounds of Asian leaders, percentage-wise, are: administration, 46%; secretariat, 22%; legal, 22%; education, 21%; social work, 3%; and military, 9%. Of course, there are significant differences between countries.

Several reasons account for the lack of business experience among senior government decision makers. First, the great effort required

to achieve political independence (Indonesia, India, Pakistan, Malaysia) has brought into government individuals with a strong background in politics. Second, in many Asian countries business is not viewed as an "honorable" profession comparable to some form of public service (the civil service or the armed forces, medicine, law, or education). Foreign enterprise originating largely from the colonizing country and from alien minority groups (for example, Chinese and Indians in Southeast Asia) is viewed often as a form of economic imperialism working to maintain the status quo of a foreign power. As a result of the foregoing reasons, key decision makers in the governments of developing Asian countries have viewed the motives and methods of businessmen as a hindrance to the economic and political development of their nations. This attitude persists because many of the current key decision makers are the very leaders who were in the forefront of the independence movements.

The attitude toward businessmen by key Asian decision makers has major implications for the foreign investor. First, the government is the key agent for change and the center of power. A foreign investor may argue that he behaves better than the indigenous businessman because he pays his taxes promptly; however, his argument may be meaningless to someone who considers that business is not a respectable occupation. Second, an existing attitude of suspicion and distrust towards business has come into being over a long period of time and is reinforced to a large extent by social and religious tradition. Hence, it cannot be changed over the short term. Third, U.S. executives, especially those at the top levels of large international enterprises, do not fully understand the nature and relative importance of non-economic forces

11

which influence the actions and policies of their counterparts in Asian governments. Similarly, government officials have a limited understanding of the economic principles which influence the policies and decisions of corporate executives.

THE NEW GENERATION

The characteristics of the demographic patterns of Asia are of critical importance in the evolution of social and economic policies of Asian countries and in the evaluation of the role of foreign enterprise. More than half of the present population of Asia was born after the Second World War, and, in many countries, after political independence had been attained. Therefore, the world view of the new generation is significantly different from that of the present group of senior decision makers, who belong to the pre-war and pre-independence generation. And they, in turn, will be replaced over the next decade by individuals from the new generation.

Table 6 offers data on the absolute numbers of people who are in the 0-24 age group in several Asian countries. It is important to note from Table 6 the absolute numbers of the new generation. In India, Pakistan, and Indonesia, the number of people under 24 years of age in 1970 was 329 million, 81 million, and 70 million, respectively. Out of sheer numbers, the younger generation has already become a major political force which will become more powerful in the coming decade.

In what ways are the attitudes of the new generation toward private foreign investments likely to differ from those of their elders? The answer to this question involves a large degree of speculation, and only broad tendencies likely to emerge can be identified. In fact, the

specific policies and programs of action are unknown even to the emerging group of decision makers.

TABLE 6

THE NEW GENERATION IN TOTAL ASIAN POPULATION--1970

Country	Total	0-24 Years of Age
Japan	101,465,000	42,920,000 (42.3%)
South Korea	33,119,000	20,567,000 (62.1%)
India	543,200,000	329,179,000 (65.5%)
Pakistan	134,000,000	81,204,000 (65.5%)
Indonesia	118,250,000	70,950,000 (65.5%)
Malaysia	13,251,000	7,951,000 (65.5%)
Thailand	36,311,000	21,787,000 (76.5%)
Philippines	38,432,000	23,059,000 (76.6%)

Source: United Nations

First, the new elites will not grant special privileges to former colonizing countries for the simple reason that they have been reared in a different environmental context. Thus, the American investor will find a less favorable atmosphere in the Philippines than he has found in the past. In fact, major changes are already underway as a result of the approaching expiration date (in 1974) of the Laurel-Langley Agreement. Similarly, in South Korea (where Americans are regarded as "number one" foreigners), with memories of the Korean War fading and the growing recognition of an imminent reduction if not total withdrawal of American military forces, the often informal and tacit privileges granted to American companies will become more infrequent and limited.

Second, the existing group of political leaders in Asia have been influenced by Western political philosophy, in many cases during their residence in Europe and the United States. Upon returning to their homeland, they stress the attainment of political independence and introduce more advanced (largely Western) styles of political life. The new generation of decision makers has far greater exposure to the West through personal visits, interactions with Western visitors, and through trade, television, and print. However, they emphasize acquiring and introducing Western skills of resource development (technology, organizational know-how) within the indigenous social-cultural-political framework. In brief, they will have more of the technocrat in them than of the political ideologist.

Third, for the foregoing reason, the Asian governments of the future will undertake a more detailed and sophisticated analysis of the potential contribution of private foreign investments to their countries. The new generation of decision makers is more pragmatic and is better trained in the social and physical sciences than their predecessors. Therefore, host government officials and foreign investors will be able to achieve greater agreement on the various technical aspects of a project. In this respect, the interaction process between the foreign investor and the host government is likely to become less emotional. However, agreement on the nature of the inputs will not mean that the two sides agree on the relative value of foreign investments. For example, differences between a foreign investor and the host government will increase on issues such as reinvestment, extent of foreign ownership, and commitment to national goals.

JAPAN AND ASIA

Any discussion of the foreign investment climate in Asia must recognize the Japanese presence in Asia. Japanese companies have many advantages over the American investor in the developing countries of Asia for the following reasons:

First, the Japanese have a good knowledge of Asia because they are Asians.

Second, Japanese investors are gaining greater acceptance in the developing countries of Asia. Understandably, the older generation still harbors some fear and resentment of the Japanese; however, the new generation is more objective in their dealings with them.

TABLE 7

WORLDWIDE DISTRIBUTION OF JAPANESE INVESTMENTS, 1969

Area	$(millions)	%
North America	$594	30.1%
Central and South America	414	20.9
Southeast Asia*	355	18.0
Middle East	268	13.6
Europe	210	10.7
Oceania	70	3.7
Africa	60	3.0
Total	$1,971	100.0%

*Korea, Taiwan, Hong Kong, the Philippines, Singapore, Indonesia, Malaysia, Thailand, India, Pakistan, Ceylon, Indochina.

Source: *White Paper on Economic Cooperation*, Ministry of International Trade and Industry, 1969, p. 477.

Third, investments in Asia account for 18% of Japanese private foreign investments (see Table 7)—a percentage which far exceeds U.S. foreign direct investment. Additionally, Japanese investors have established a far greater number of projects in Asia than in any other part of the world. As a result, it is to be expected that the Japanese will invest further in Asian markets.

Fourth, the bulk of Japanese aid goes to the developing countries of Asia. As this aid grows, Japanese companies will benefit directly (by providing plant, equipment, technology) and indirectly (by increasing their bargaining position, viz., through the resulting good will).

1

Nature of the Study

OBJECTIVES

The objectives of this study are:

a) To present the viewpoint of American executives on the essential features of the foreign investment climate in eight Asian countries at present and in five years.

b) To highlight the policy implications of the response for foreign companies and for host governments.

More specifically, the questions in this study deal with--

1) <u>Foreign investment objectives</u>: What are the main investment objectives of American companies in Asia?

2) <u>Political stability</u>: How stable are the governments of Asian countries at present and in five years? What will be the primary reasons for change?

3) <u>Foreign ownership</u>: What is the present attitude of Asian governments toward foreign ownership? What will be the attitude of Asian governments in five years? What is the extent of American ownership in Asia? What do executives anticipate in five years? To what extent do foreign companies and host governments in Asia differ on the question of extent of foreign ownership?

4) <u>Types of investment</u>: What types of investments do American companies have at present in Asia? What types do executives anticipate having in five years? What types of investment are preferred by Asian governments? What are likely to be the differences between Asian govern-

17

ments and American companies regarding types of investments?

5) <u>Use of expatriates</u>: What is the attitude of Asian countries toward the use of foreign nationals in senior management positions? To what extent are foreign companies compelled to use nationals for such positions? Which positions in senior management are foreign companies likely to assign to nationals, and why?

6) <u>Operating difficulties</u>: What are the main operating problems faced by foreign companies? Are the operating problems at an acceptable level of difficulty or not?

7) <u>Japanese competition in Asia</u>: What is the extent of Japanese competition in Asia? Why are the Japanese such strong competitors?

8) <u>Future investment plans</u>: Do American companies plan to increase, decrease, or maintain at the same level their investments in Asia? Where and how will changes occur?

METHODOLOGY

A ten-page questionnaire with seventeen detailed questions was mailed to a group of selected companies. Appendix B presents the final questionnaire and additional details on the research methodology. A total of 421 questionnaires were mailed on the second and third Fridays in April, 1971, to either the vice-president international or the chief operating officers of American companies with operations in Asia. Ninety-four questionnaires were returned for a response rate of 22%.

POSITION OF RESPONDENTS

The breakdown of responding executives is as follows:

Vice Chairman	1
President	10
Vice President	16
Director, General Mgr., Regional Mgr., Mgr. International Operations, Export Marketing Mgr.	25
Controller, Treasurer	3
Ass't. to Pres., Ass't. V.P., Ass't. Regional Mgr., Administrative Mgr., Supervisor, Ass't. Secretary, Ass't. Mgr., Operations Research Analyst	10
Respondent did not give his title	29
Total	94

PROFILE OF RESPONDING COMPANIES

This section offers a profile of the 94 responding companies by product group, sales volume, extent of overseas and Asian sales and profits, distribution of operations by country, types of operations, and objectives of Asian operations of American companies.

Product Group. The response is from companies mainly involved in manufacturing operations, and in this respect it is significantly greater than the distribution of U.S. investments in Asia as revealed in Table 4. The breakdown by SITC* product groups follows:

Group	*No. of Respondents*
Food and Live Animals	3
Beverages and Tobacco	1
Crude Materials, Inedible, except Fuels	2
Minerals Fuels, **Lubricants**, and Related Materials	2
Animals and Vegetable Oils and Fats	1
Chemicals	17
Manufactured Goods Classified Chiefly by Materials	18
Machinery and Transport Equipment	26
Miscellaneous Manufactured Articles	11
Service	10
Product not listed by Respondent	3
Total	94

---

* Standard International Trade Classification

The reason why there is an emphasis on manufacturing investments is the policy of Asian governments to secure greater foreign investments in manufacturing. Also, it follows that companies with only sales offices or distributorships and companies in the extractive industries in search of new and profitable investment opportunities are likely in the future to invest in manufacturing.

Annual Corporate Sales Volume. The annual corporate sales volume of respondents ranged from less than $200 million to over $2 billion (see Graph 1). The single largest category of respondents were the relatively small companies (less than $200 million annual sales) accounting for 39% of all respondents. The second largest category was of medium-size companies (between $200 and $600 million annual sales) accounting for 25% of the response, followed by large companies (between $601 and $2,000 million) with 27% of the response and giant companies (over $2,000 million) with 9% of the response.

Overseas Sales and Profits. Graph 2 shows the percentage distribution of responding companies' overseas sales and profits in 1970 as a percent of 1970 total corporate sales and profits. This measure suggests the relative importance of international business activities for the responding companies.

A significant minority (12%) of the responding companies derive over 50% of the annual corporate sales from overseas operations. Another 31% derive between 26-50%, while 35% derive between 11-26% of annual corporate sales from overseas operations. But 21% of the respondents derive less than 11% of overall corporate sales from overseas operations.

Profits from overseas operations account for varying levels of annual

GRAPH 1

DISTRIBUTION OF RESPONDING COMPANIES' 1970 CORPORATE SALES

N=92

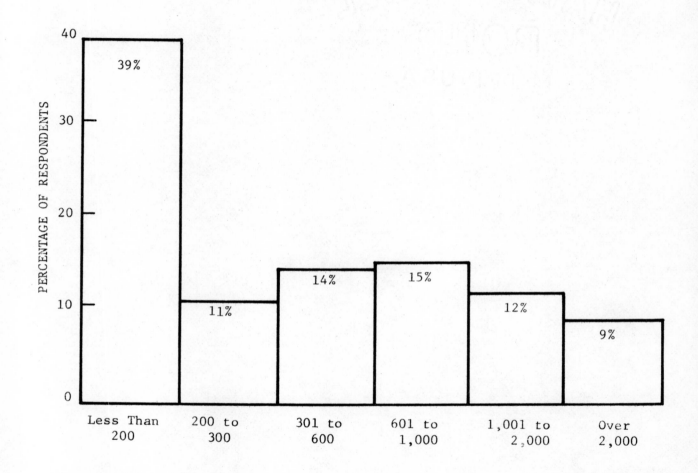

1970 ANNUAL CORPORATE SALES IN MILLIONS OF DOLLARS

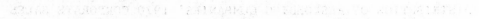

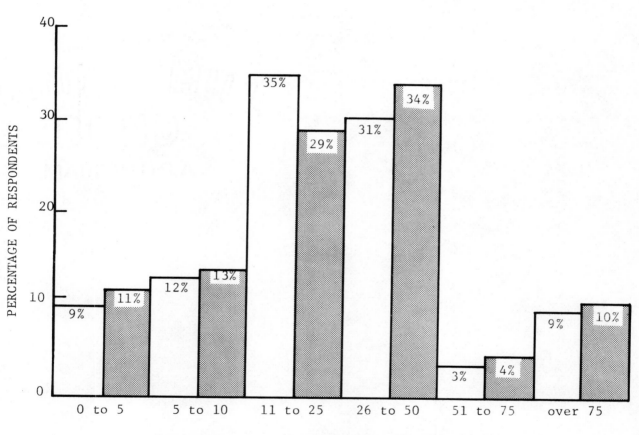

GRAPH **2**

DISTRIBUTION OF RESPONDING COMPANIES' OVERSEAS
SALES AND PROFITS IN **1970** AS A PERCENTAGE
OF 1970 TOTAL CORPORATE SALES AND PROFITS

N=89   (sales)
N=80   (profits)

PERCENTAGE OF RESPONDENTS

PERCENTAGE DERIVED FROM OVERSEAS OPERATIONS

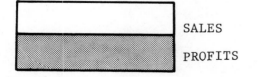

SALES

PROFITS

PERCENTAGE FIGURES MAY NOT ADD
TO 100% BECAUSE OF ROUNDING

corporate profits. While roughly 24% derive less than 10% of annual profits from overseas operations, another 14% derive more than 50% from overseas operations. The majority of the responding companies, nearly 63%, secure between 11% and 50% of annual corporate profits from overseas operations. Thus, for the large majority of responding companies, overseas operations are important while for some they are a critical component in overall corporate sales. These companies are the ones more likely to extend their operations into Asia than companies without any or with very limited international operations.

Asian Sales and Profits. Graph 3 shows the percent of annual corporate sales and profits derived from Asian operations. Roughly 32% of the responding firms secured 2% or less in annual sales from Asian operations while 36% secured between 2 and 6%. Another 21% derived between 6 and 15%, and 11% derived over 15% of annual corporate sales from Asian operations. The highest percentage response (22%) is for the 3-6% category followed by 21% in the 6-15% category. Thus, Asian sales are important for a significant percentage of the responding companies.

Nearly 47% of the responding companies derive 3% or less of annual corporate profits from Asian operations, 18% are in the 3-6% category, 21% in the 6-15% category and 15% are in the over 15% category. The highest response is for the 0-1% category followed by 6-15% and 3-6% categories. It appears that the contribution of Asian operations to overall corporate profits is either minimal or tends to be fairly significant. Nearly 37% of the responding companies derive 6% or more of annual corporate profits from Asian operations.

Operations by Country. Graph 4 shows the distribution by country of Asian

GRAPH 3

DISTRIBUTION OF RESPONDING COMPANIES' ASIAN
SALES AND PROFITS IN 1970 AS A PERCENTAGE OF
1970 TOTAL CORPORATE SALES AND PROFITS

N=81 (sales)
N=74 (profits)

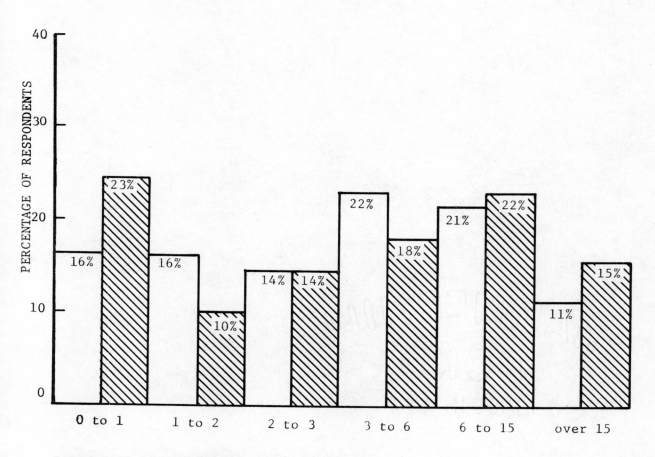

PERCENTAGE DERIVED FROM ASIAN OPERATIONS

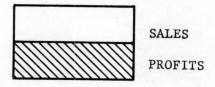

SALES

PROFITS

24

operations of the responding companies. By far the largest number of operations are maintained in Japan, as noted by 90% of the responding companies. In 1969 Japan accounted for over 36% of total U.S. direct investment in Asia. The Philippines, with its close historical ties to the U.S., has the second largest number of operations, noted by 64% of the respondents, followed by India (55%), Thailand (54%), South Korea (47%), Taiwan (46%), Malaysia (40%), and Indonesia (28%). The distribution of the responding companies by the eight countries in the survey shows that they have experience in one or more of the countries in the Asian region included in the survey.

Type of Operations. Graph 5 shows the Asian distribution by country and type of investment of the responding companies. The operations should be viewed from the standpoint of commitment by the foreign investor-- from distributorships to manufacturing. A company often engages in several types of investment at the same time. It can undertake manufacturing in a country through a joint venture or a wholly-owned subsidiary by licensing its trade mark and patents and by supplying the technical know-how; it can also enter into a management services contract for an agreed period of time to ensure effective development of operations. Furthermore, it can maintain sales offices in important markets while creating a network of distributors in others. In brief, the different types of operations are interrelated. Graph 5 clearly indicates that companies maintain several types of operations at the same time. If they have a high-commitment type of investment (e.g., wholly-owned subsidiary for manufacturing), they will nearly always maintain also some form of low-commitment investment (e.g., sales office). Additionally, for companies with essentially low-commitment investments, the tendency often

GRAPH 4

DISTRIBUTION OF RESPONDING COMPANIES'
ASIAN INVESTMENT

N=89

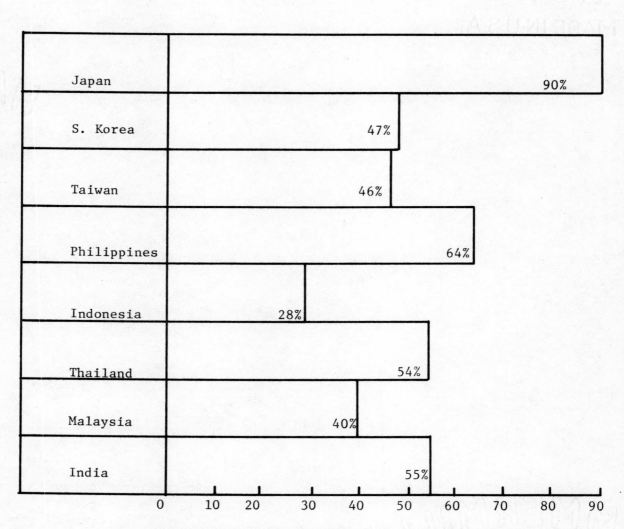

PERCENTAGE OF RESPONDENTS INVESTED IN EACH COUNTRY

GRAPH 5

DISTRIBUTION OF RESPONDING COMPANIES' TYPES
OF OPERATIONS IN ASIA

Types of
Operations

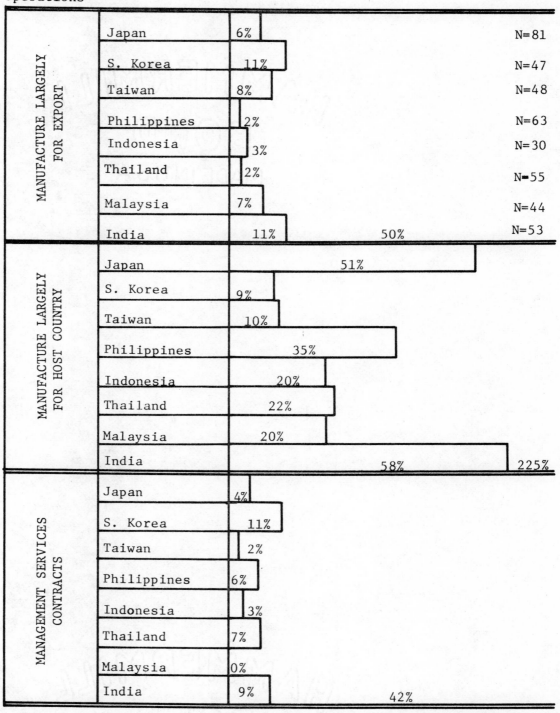

GRAPH 5 (continued)

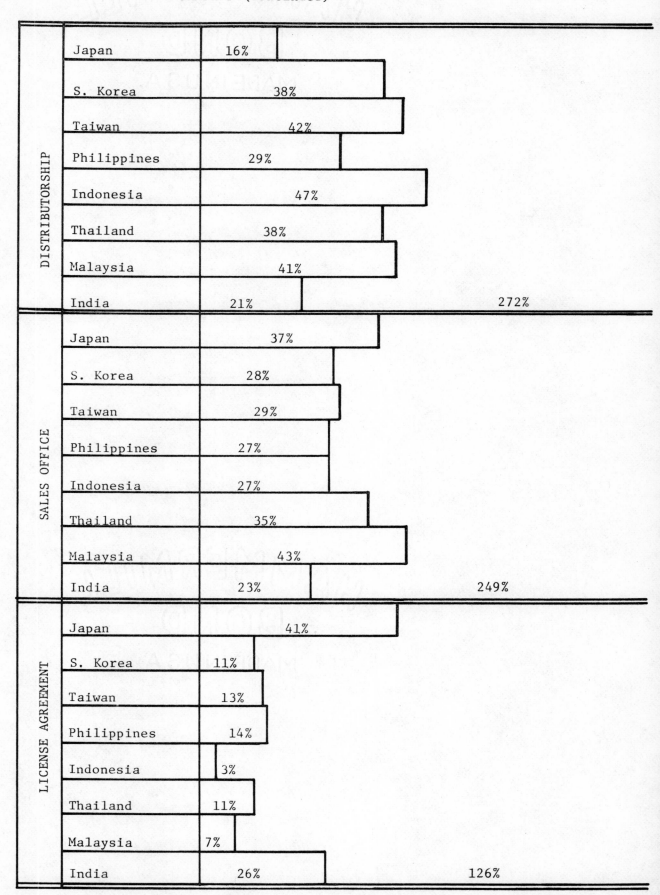

DISTRIBUTORSHIP

Country	Percent
Japan	16%
S. Korea	38%
Taiwan	42%
Philippines	29%
Indonesia	47%
Thailand	38%
Malaysia	41%
India	21%

272%

SALES OFFICE

Country	Percent
Japan	37%
S. Korea	28%
Taiwan	29%
Philippines	27%
Indonesia	27%
Thailand	35%
Malaysia	43%
India	23%

249%

LICENSE AGREEMENT

Country	Percent
Japan	41%
S. Korea	11%
Taiwan	13%
Philippines	14%
Indonesia	3%
Thailand	11%
Malaysia	7%
India	26%

126%

GRAPH 5 (continued)

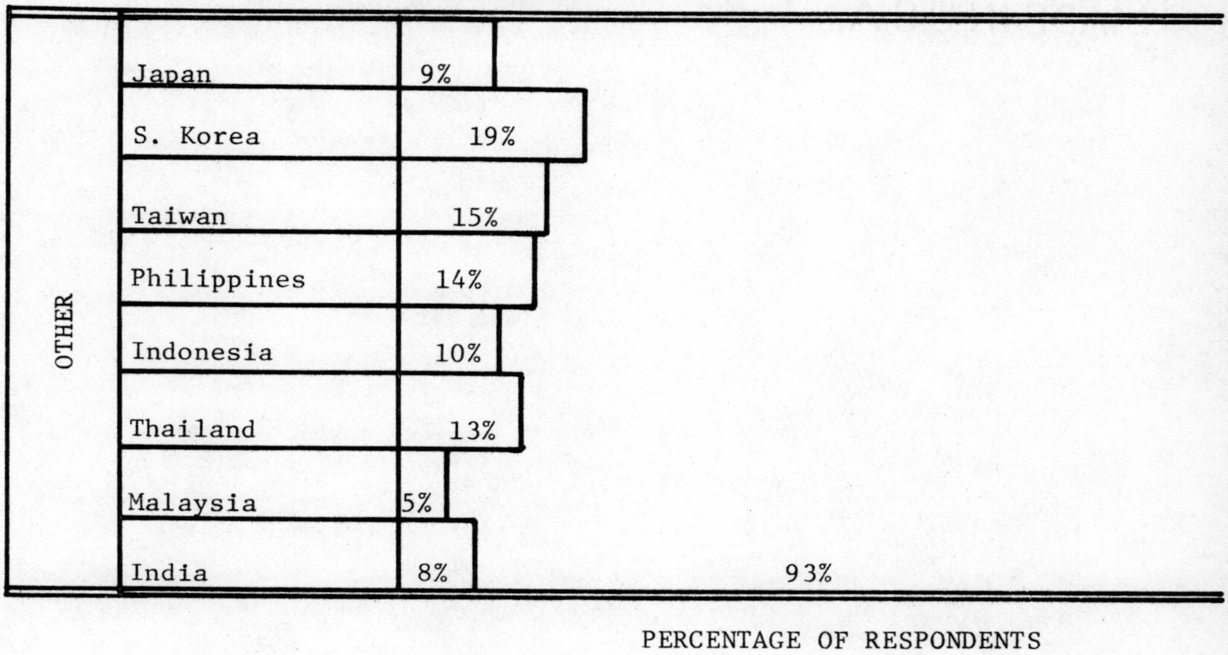

OTHER		
Japan	9%	
S. Korea	19%	
Taiwan	15%	
Philippines	14%	
Indonesia	10%	
Thailand	13%	
Malaysia	5%	
India	8%	93%

PERCENTAGE OF RESPONDENTS

TOTAL FOR A COUNTRY MAY EXCEED 100% BECAUSE SOME
RESPONDENTS HAVE MORE THAN ONE TYPE OF OPERATION
IN THAT COUNTRY

is to move toward high-commitment investments (e.g., from distributor-ship to sales office to licensing to manufacturing). Of course, a company can leapfrog stages and move directly from distributorship to manufacturing.

There are significant variations in types of operations maintained by American companies in Asian countries. Foreign investments in Japan are in manufacturing largely for the host-country market. The buying potential of the Japanese market explains this preference. License agreements are the second most frequent response category, indicating the Japanese preference for acquiring foreign technology and know-how rather than foreign equity investments. American companies thus reduce their commercial risk by gradually increasing their level of commitment. The third most frequent response category is sales office, which is explained by the difficulties of entering the Japanese market and the desire to proceed gradually thereafter, as a company acquires greater skill in operating in the Japanese context. Distributorships are the next most frequent category of response, but it appears that respon-dents prefer to maintain sales offices over distributorships, perhaps because of the high potential of the Japanese market. Very few respon-dents view Japan as a base for export manufacturing because of high labor costs. Also, by exporting from wholly-owned operations, a compa-ny can retain all of the profits instead of sharing them with a local partner in a joint venture, as is almost invariably true in Japan. Management services contracts are used least frequently by the responding companies.

For South Korea, the greatest frequency of response was given to distributorship and sales office, in that order. Licensing agreements,

management services contracts, and manufacturing largely for exports are almost equal in frequency of response. Very few respondents manufacture solely for the host-country market because of the small size of the market and its limited purchasing power. The distribution of response for Taiwan is generally similar to that of South Korea but with a significantly smaller response under the management services contract category.

The greatest frequency of response for the Philippines fell under the category of manufacturing largely for the host country. A far lower frequency of response was recorded for license agreements. Respondents placed emphasis on distributorship and sales office. Manufacturing for export is virtually non-existent for the responding companies operating in the Philippines.

By far the largest category of response for Indonesia fell in distributorship and sales offices, with the former being far more frequent than the latter. License agreements are very limited, as are management services contracts. A significant minority of respondents have manufacturing operations in Indonesia for the domestic market, while manufacturing for exports is rare.

For Thailand, distributorship and sales offices are most frequently mentioned, followed by manufacturing largely for the local market and license agreements. Very few of the responding companies manufacture in Thailand for exporting to other countries.

In general, the pattern in Malaysia is similar to that reflected in other developing Asian countries, that is, the most frequent response falls within the categories of sales office and distributorship followed by manufacturing largely for the host-country market. Only a few

companies have considered Malaysia as a base for exporting or for licensing agreements.

The single most frequent category of response for India is manufacturing largely for the host-country market. However, in comparison, few respondents use India as a base for exports. The second largest single category of response is that of licensing agreements. This is due to the regulations imposed by the government on foreign investments. In addition, while the potential market is huge, the actual market is often limited, and companies use licensing as a means of gradually penetrating the market. The third and fourth most frequent responses fall within the categories of sales office and distributorships. Management services contracts appear to be of relatively limited use for the responding companies.

Objectives for Investing in Asia. Graph 6 presents a distribution of the objectives for investing in Asia. As expected, objectives differ by country. By far the most important objective for investing in Japan is to receive dividends and royalties through equity and licensing arrangements. There is also the desire to profit from the development of new markets in a highly industrialized country such as Japan.

Other reasons offered, in declining frequency of response, are: export to third countries from Japan, export of U.S. raw materials and semi-finished goods, export of U.S. machinery and equipment, and overcoming Japanese import restrictions. (The last reason is closely related to equity investments and licensing arrangements that offer dividends and royalties.)

The single most important objective of responding companies in

South Korea is to develop new markets; the second most important objective is to obtain dividends and royalties. Other objectives stated, in declining order of importance, are: to overcome import restrictions, to promote export of U.S. machinery and equipment, to export to the United States, and to export to third country markets from Korea.

In general, the response for Taiwan is not significantly different from that of South Korea. The most frequently stated objective is to develop new markets, followed closely by that of obtaining dividends and royalties. Other objectives in declining order are: to export to the U.S. from Taiwan, to promote exports to Taiwan of U.S. manufactured goods and equipment and of raw materials and semi-finished goods, and to overcome import restrictions into Taiwan.

For the Philippines, the order of priority of the top two objectives is reversed in comparison to South Korea and Taiwan. Thus, the most important objective is to secure dividends and royalties, followed by developing new markets in the Philippines. This preference is partly explained by the fact that American companies have been in the Philippines for a long time compared to other Asian countries. The other objectives, in declining frequency of response, are to overcome Filipino import restrictions, to promote export of U.S. raw materials and semi-finished goods and U.S. machinery and equipment, to export to third countries from the Philippines, and to export from the Philippines to the U.S.

The most frequently stated objective for Indonesia is to develop new markets, followed by securing dividends and royalties. The other objectives in order of frequency are: to overcome Indonesian import restrictions, to promote export of U.S. machinery and equipment, to

promote export of U.S. raw materials and semi-finished goods, to obtain raw materials from Indonesia, and to export to third countries and to the U.S. from Indonesia.

The top two objectives for Thailand remain the same as for the other Asian countries. However, developing new markets and obtaining dividends and royalties are the most frequently stated objectives of the responding companies. The other objectives are to overcome Thai import restrictions, to promote exports of U.S. machinery and equipment, to export to third countries from Thailand, to promote export of U.S. raw materials and semi-finished goods to Thailand, and to export to the U.S. from Thailand.

For Malaysia, developing new markets is by far the most frequently stated objective, followed by securing dividends and royalties. The other objectives are to promote exports of U.S. machinery and equipment, to overcome Malaysian import restrictions, to export to the U.S. from Malaysia, to export to third country markets from Malaysia, to promote exports of U.S. raw materials and semi-finished goods, and to export raw materials from Malaysia.

The objectives of responding companies for operations in India are somewhat different from those given for other developing countries of Asia. However, in general the basic trend remains the same. Thus, by far the most important objectives are to secure dividends and royalties and to develop new markets in India. The third most frequently stated objective is to use India as a base for exporting to third-country markets, followed by the objective of overcoming Indian import restrictions. These objectives are followed, in declining frequency of response, by: to promote exports of U.S. raw materials and semi-finished products and of U.S. machinery and equipment, and to export from India to the U.S.

GRAPH 6

DISTRIBUTION OF RESPONDING COMPANIES' KEY
OBJECTIVES FOR INVESTMENTS IN ASIA

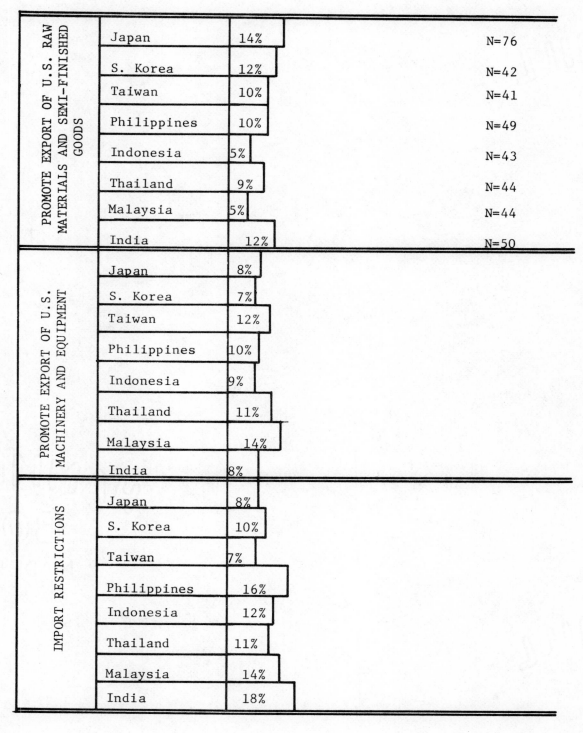

PROMOTE EXPORT OF U.S. RAW MATERIALS AND SEMI-FINISHED GOODS		
Japan	14%	N=76
S. Korea	12%	N=42
Taiwan	10%	N=41
Philippines	10%	N=49
Indonesia	5%	N=43
Thailand	9%	N=44
Malaysia	5%	N=44
India	12%	N=50

PROMOTE EXPORT OF U.S. MACHINERY AND EQUIPMENT	
Japan	8%
S. Korea	7%
Taiwan	12%
Philippines	10%
Indonesia	9%
Thailand	11%
Malaysia	14%
India	8%

IMPORT RESTRICTIONS	
Japan	8%
S. Korea	10%
Taiwan	7%
Philippines	16%
Indonesia	12%
Thailand	11%
Malaysia	14%
India	18%

GRAPH 6 (continued)

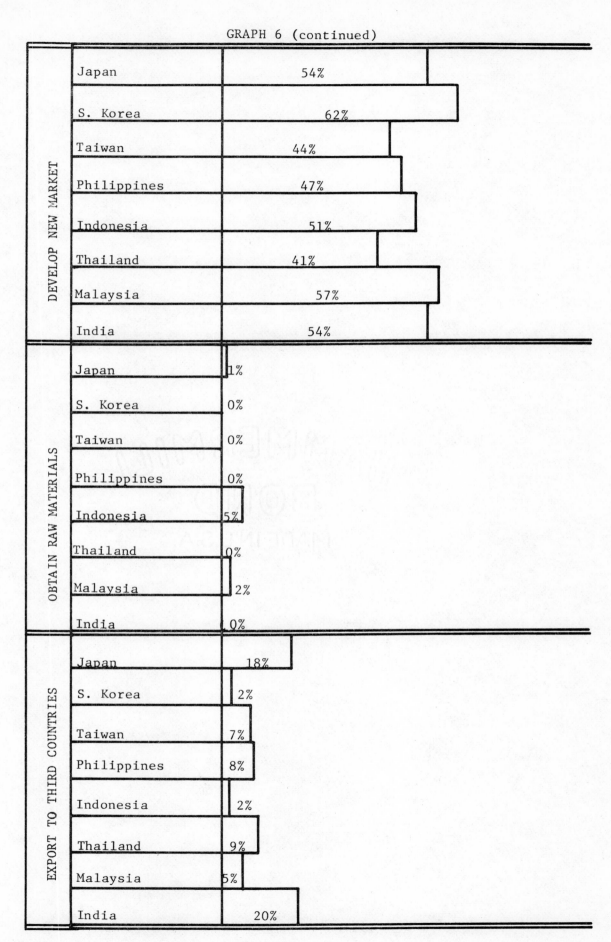

DEVELOP NEW MARKET

Japan	54%
S. Korea	62%
Taiwan	44%
Philippines	47%
Indonesia	51%
Thailand	41%
Malaysia	57%
India	54%

OBTAIN RAW MATERIALS

Japan	1%
S. Korea	0%
Taiwan	0%
Philippines	0%
Indonesia	5%
Thailand	0%
Malaysia	2%
India	0%

EXPORT TO THIRD COUNTRIES

Japan	18%
S. Korea	2%
Taiwan	7%
Philippines	8%
Indonesia	2%
Thailand	9%
Malaysia	5%
India	20%

GRAPH 6 (continued)

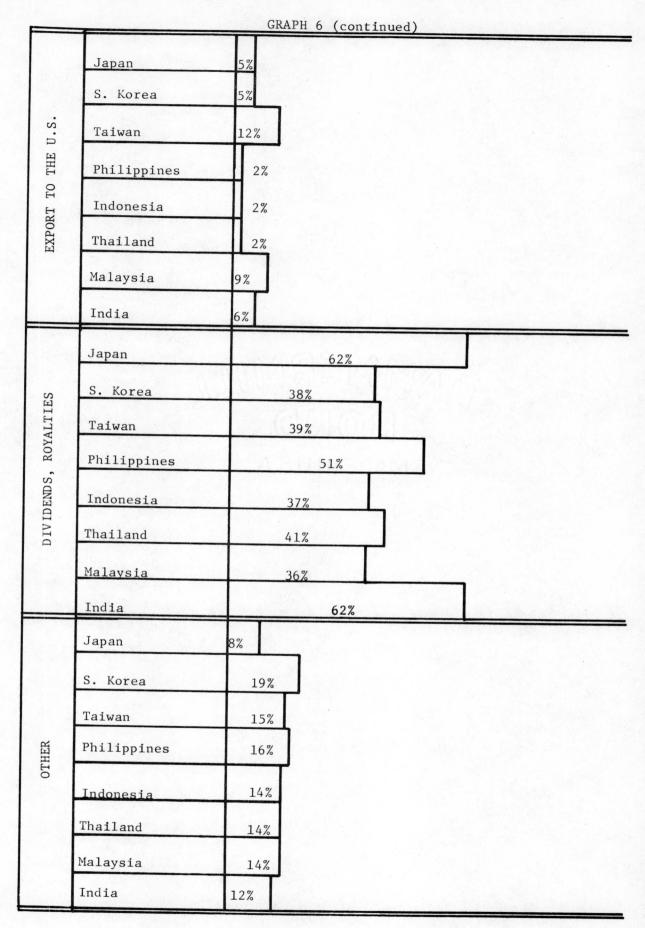

EXPORT TO THE U.S.

Japan	5%
S. Korea	5%
Taiwan	12%
Philippines	2%
Indonesia	2%
Thailand	2%
Malaysia	9%
India	6%

DIVIDENDS, ROYALTIES

Japan	62%
S. Korea	38%
Taiwan	39%
Philippines	51%
Indonesia	37%
Thailand	41%
Malaysia	36%
India	62%

OTHER

Japan	8%
S. Korea	19%
Taiwan	15%
Philippines	16%
Indonesia	14%
Thailand	14%
Malaysia	14%
India	12%

The emphasis on developing new markets in Asian countries is indicative of a relatively long-term approach being adopted by the responding companies. The emphasis on dividends and royalties suggests that companies are stressing higher commitment types of investments (e.g., equity, licensing). Exporting from Asian countries within or outside of the Asian area does not appear to be a significant objective of the responding companies.

2
The Political Environment

Government stability is the single most important prerequisite for investing abroad. But "stability" is variously defined, depending on the experience of the investor. Thus, an American may consider a country unstable given the recurrence of certain events which would not seem normal at home, such as a rapid shift of ministers or public demonstrations that receive inordinate publicity through the press or television. Yet, those events may be "normal" for a country if they are part and parcel of its political and social life.

Many major political events have occurred in Asia in the recent past. During 1971, several Asian countries held elections (India, South Korea, Indonesia, Pakistan), and even in countries with strong leaders--Prime Minister Indira Gandhi in India, President Suharto in Indonesia--foreign companies are uncertain about policies pertaining to economic development and foreign enterprise.

Political unrest is another characteristic of Asian countries. The Constitutional Referendum in the Philippines, the race riots in Malaysia, the religious conflicts in India, the Communist threat in Thailand and Indonesia, the Pakistani revolt that culminated in the formation of the separate sovereign state of Bangladesh, the conflict in Indochina--these are serious political events whose effect on the investment climate is hard to determine.

The general reduction of America's military presence in Vietnam, Thailand, and South Korea may influence the policies that these countries will follow in the future toward the United States, and the privileges (often tacit) extended to American investors are likely to be greatly reduced. The recent dramatic rapport between the United States and Mainland China (The People's Republic of China) has affected the political relationships between other Asian countries and Mainland China and between Asian countries and the United States. The prime example, of course, is Japan, which is making a serious and undisguised effort to court Mainland China for political and economic reasons. South Korea and Thailand, who have been staunch U.S. allies, will have to seriously revaluate their position toward the Mainland Chinese. The initial moves of such a process have been reflected in the recent agreement by North and South Korea to avoid hostilities. The largest single effect, however, has been on Taiwan, which has already lost its seat in the United Nations.

This chapter presents the views of the responding companies on the relative stability of Asian governments at present and in five years. Graphs 7 and 8 present the opinions of executives, and Graph 9 offers a distribution of possible causes of change in the stability of Asian governments in five years.

It should be noted that not a single respondent regards any of the Asian countries to be highly unstable. And, except for the Philippines, the overwhelming majority of respondents do not regard the Asian countries to be unstable.

It is reasonable to assume that Asia as a region compares very favorably with other developing regions of the world in terms of govern-

mental stability. However, the relative political stability among Asian countries is seen to vary greatly.

ANALYSIS BY COUNTRY

Japan. Japan is considered to be strongly stable at present and highly stable in the next five years as a result of the economic stability of the country (see Graph 7). Also affecting favorably Japan's stability are a greater sense of national unity of the Japanese people and consolidation of power by political leaders. Overall, forces contributing to stability of the Japanese government are far more powerful and pronounced than those leading to instability.

South Korea. South Korea is considered a stable country by the majority of the respondents; many consider it as being only moderately stable. No significant change is expected over the next five years. However, a few view South Korea as moving toward the moderately unstable category. South Korea's stability is seen as the result of economic stability, consolidation of power by political leaders, and a greater sense of national unity.

Taiwan. Taiwan is considered to be a stable country by the majority; a few place it in the moderately stable and highly stable categories. However, significant changes are expected over the next five years, as shown in Graph 9, with a marked decline in the stable and highly stable categories and a noticeable increase in the moderately unstable category. (Of course, the recent U.S. rapprochement with Mainland China and Taiwan's

expulsion from the United Nations are events which are bound to affect its stability.)

The single most important reason contributing to political stability is the country's economic stability, followed by consolidation of power by political leaders. Among the forces contributing to Taiwan's instability are the increasing strength of political opposition groups and a growing social unrest. (Both these forces are likely to increase as a result of Taiwan's new position in the international context and in particular as a result of the dramatic change in the policies of the U.S. and Japanese governments toward Taiwan and Mainland China.)

The Philippines. The Filipino government is considered to be the least stable of any of the Asian governments at present. A majority consider the Philippines to be moderately stable with a decrease in stability in five years. A minority view it as unstable and expect it to worsen in the next five years. (The impending expiration of the Laurel-Langley Agreement is an important cause for anxiety on the part of American companies.)

Unlike Japan, where a small minority of respondents consider that increasing political opposition contributes to political stability, in the Philippines the same factor is interpreted as contributing to instability. This is an important observation on the relative political and economic maturity of a country (the Philippines versus Japan), and it shows that "stability" is the result of many factors which have to be viewed in relation to the total environment.

The single most important reason for the increasing instability

of the Filipino government is social unrest in the country. It appears
that the responding companies expect the current level of social unrest
to escalate with adverse consequences on the stability of the government.

Indonesia. Indonesia is considered to be moderately stable followed by
moderately unstable. An increase in stability is expected in the next
five years. No single reason is accountable for this development.
Governmental stability is seen to increase as a result of economic stability, consolidation of power by political leaders, and a greater sense
of national unity. However, two reasons contributing to governmental
instability are increasing social unrest and increasing strength of
political opposition groups. The recent elections in Indonesia have
greatly strengthened President Suharto's government, which is likely to
continue with the broad range of economic development policies it has
pursued in the past. And the opposition of local groups is far less
significant than it was before the elections.

Malaysia. Malaysia at present is considered moderately stable, followed
by stable. In five years, respondents anticipate a move toward greater
stability.

As in the case of other Asian countries, Malaysia's stability is
viewed as the result of economic stability, greater sense of national
unity, and consolidation of power by political leaders. However, a significant minority referred to increasing social unrest and increasing
strength of political opposition groups as contributing to future governmental instability. The violent race riots of May 1969 in Malaysia
exemplify the intense racial conflicts in the country. The coming years

43

will show whether the politically powerful Malays and the economically dominant Chinese are able to achieve an effective sharing of powers and roles.

India. India is seen as moderately stable by the majority; a few consider it stable. Respondents anticipate a slight decrease in stability in the next five years. (However, the recent elections in India and the military victory over Pakistan have given Prime Minister Gandhi's government considerable power, and the stability of the government is far greater than at the time the questionnaire was circulated.)

A major reason for the increase in governmental stability is consolidation of power by political leaders. A minority feels that economic stability through agricultural and industrial development would help reduce governmental instability. Nevertheless, respondents believe that increasing social unrest and the increasing strength of political opposition groups will adversely affect India's political stability.

The most important reason for maintaining or reducing the rate of governmental instability is economic. This reason is applicable to all the Asian countries surveyed with the exception of India and Indonesia, where consolidation of power by political leaders is viewed as the main reason. Conversely, governmental instability in Asia is viewed as the result of increasing social unrest and the increasing strength of political opposition groups.

IMPLICATIONS FOR FOREIGN COMPANIES

Asia as a region does not receive a "negative" rating on governmental stablility, with the possible exception of the Philippines. While

GRAPH 7

DISTRIBUTION OF RESPONDENTS' OPINIONS OF
ASIAN GOVERNMENTS' STABILITY IN 1971

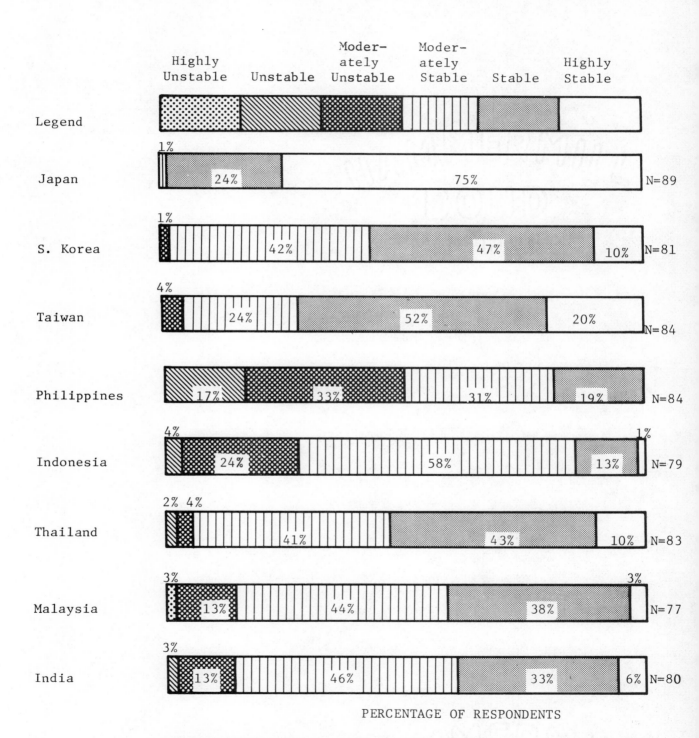

PERCENTAGE OF RESPONDENTS

TOTALS MAY NOT ADD TO 100% BECAUSE OF ROUNDING

GRAPH 8

DISTRIBUTION OF RESPONDENTS' OPINIONS OF ASIAN GOVERNMENTS' STABILITY IN 1976

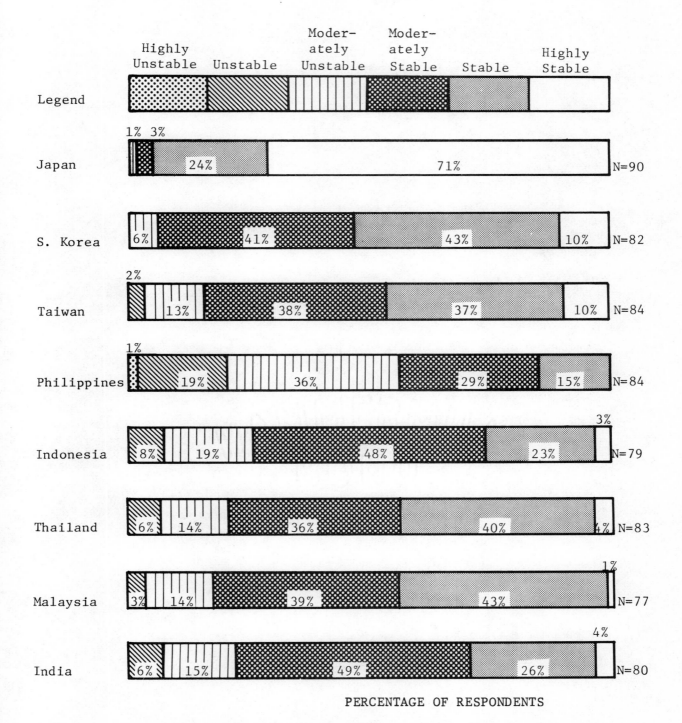

PERCENTAGE OF RESPONDENTS

TOTALS MAY NOT ADD TO 100% BECAUSE OF ROUNDING

46

GRAPH 9

DISTRIBUTION OF RESPONDENTS' PRIMARY REASONS FOR THEIR
OPINIONS ABOUT ASIAN GOVERNMENTS' STABILITY IN 1976

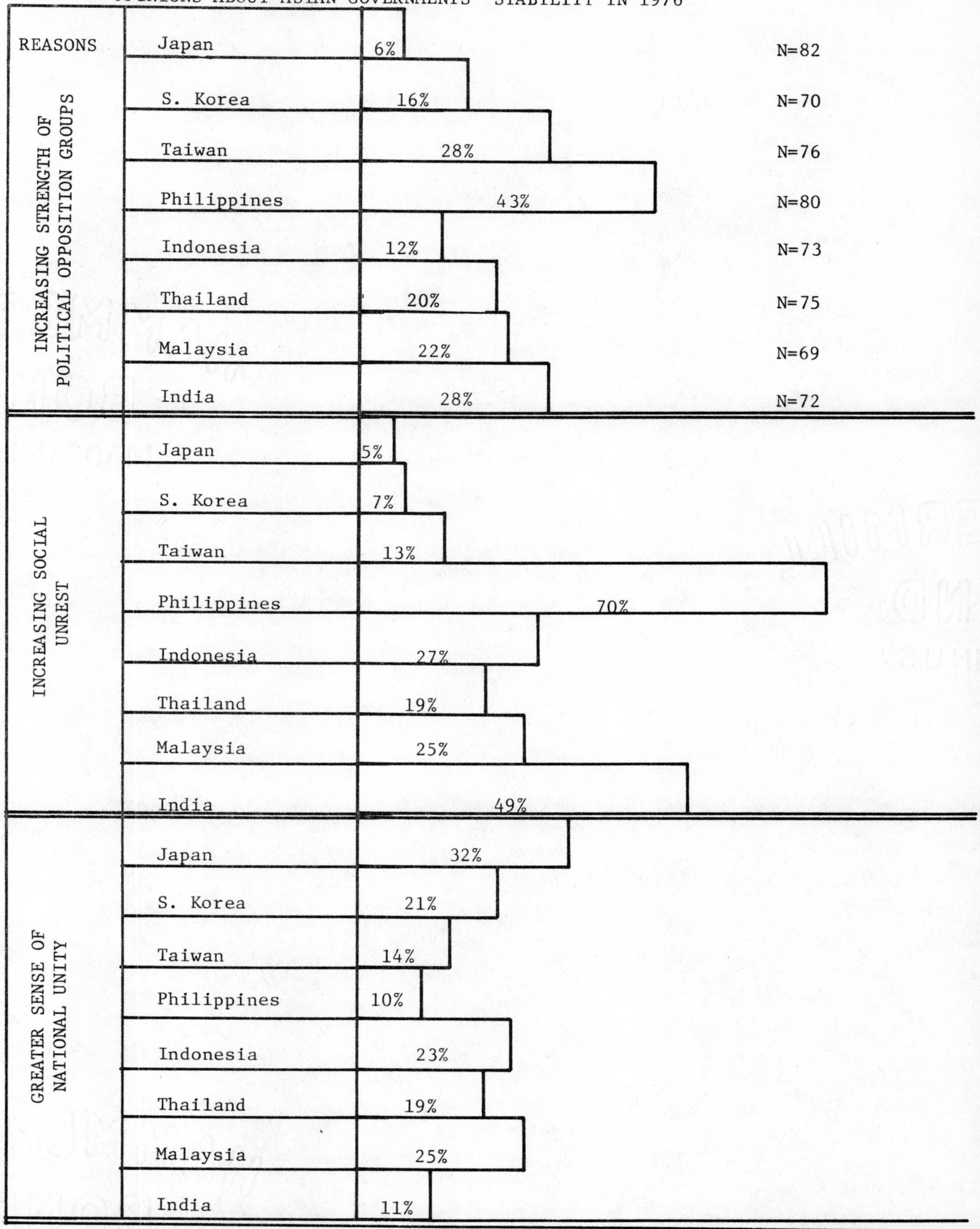

INCREASING STRENGTH OF POLITICAL OPPOSITION GROUPS

Country	%	N
Japan	6%	N=82
S. Korea	16%	N=70
Taiwan	28%	N=76
Philippines	43%	N=80
Indonesia	12%	N=73
Thailand	20%	N=75
Malaysia	22%	N=69
India	28%	N=72

INCREASING SOCIAL UNREST

Country	%
Japan	5%
S. Korea	7%
Taiwan	13%
Philippines	70%
Indonesia	27%
Thailand	19%
Malaysia	25%
India	49%

GREATER SENSE OF NATIONAL UNITY

Country	%
Japan	32%
S. Korea	21%
Taiwan	14%
Philippines	10%
Indonesia	23%
Thailand	19%
Malaysia	25%
India	11%

GRAPH 9 (continued)

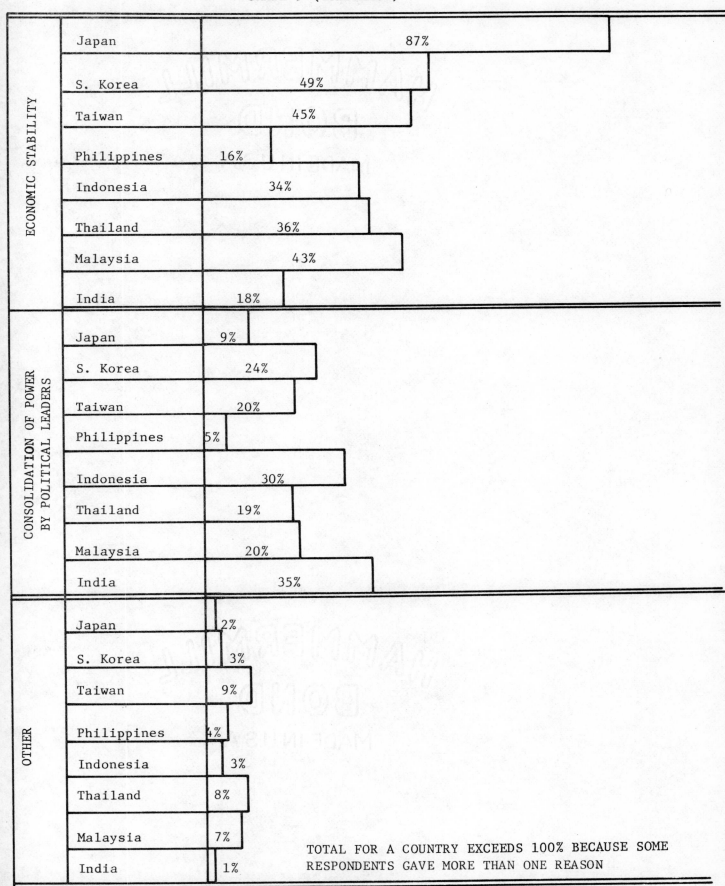

ECONOMIC STABILITY	
Japan	87%
S. Korea	49%
Taiwan	45%
Philippines	16%
Indonesia	34%
Thailand	36%
Malaysia	43%
India	18%

CONSOLIDATION OF POWER BY POLITICAL LEADERS	
Japan	9%
S. Korea	24%
Taiwan	20%
Philippines	5%
Indonesia	30%
Thailand	19%
Malaysia	20%
India	35%

OTHER	
Japan	2%
S. Korea	3%
Taiwan	9%
Philippines	4%
Indonesia	3%
Thailand	8%
Malaysia	7%
India	1%

TOTAL FOR A COUNTRY EXCEEDS 100% BECAUSE SOME
RESPONDENTS GAVE MORE THAN ONE REASON

comparative data does not exist for the developing countries of the Middle East, Africa, and Latin America, it is safe to assume that over-all governmental stability in Asia is at least as good as, if not better than, the stability of other developing regions.

In addition, two characteristics promoting political stability augur well for foreign companies investing in Asia. The first one is economic. Governments are aware of the necessity for achieving acceptable levels of economic gains for their people; otherwise their positions are in jeopardy. As a consequence, foreign companies have had and will continue to have a role to play within this broader context of government objectives in order to achieve some acceptable level of economic growth.

Second, the emergence of political leaders with greater political power (such as President Park Chung Hee in South Korea, President Suharto in Indonesia, and Prime Minister Indira Gandhi in India) is likely to encourage them to devote more attention, and adopt a pragmatic approach, to economic matters.

The American businessman, conditioned by his own political system and its stability, often regards foreign political situations as dangerous because they do not conform to his norm. Therefore, the measures of political stability offered here might be interpreted in an even more positive sense if the norms and measures of stability are not those applicable in the U.S. but those found in Asia.

3

FOREIGN OWNERSHIP POLICIES

The extent of ownership permitted by host governments is an important consideration in the decision of a company to invest abroad. This is particularly true in the case of the multinational enterprise which seeks control over its worldwide operations in order to secure the most effective level of performance on a worldwide basis. However, host countries, both developed and developing, impose numerous restrictions on the extent of foreign ownership they will allow. In developing countries such an attitude may be the result of a colonial past, a desire to have control in the hands of nationals, and an effort to develop talent (versus a dependence on foreign skills).

Japan and the developing countries of Asia have numerous policies on extent of foreign ownership, and the exact interpretation of these policies tends to vary by the nature of the investment. Thus, technology-intensive investments (e.g., integrated circuits) largely for export purposes are strongly favored, and in such cases the foreign investor is often permitted to have 100% ownership. In less attractive types of investments, host governments adopt a far more stringent attitude on the extent of foreign ownership.

The objectives of this chapter are to present the ownership policies of responding companies, the existing ownership configurations, and the

changes companies anticipate making in five years. This chapter also presents the views of responding companies on what they expect to be the attitudes of Asian governments toward extent of foreign ownership at present and in five years, and the main reasons for the changes expected.

A comparison of company policies and attitudes of host governments will reveal the extent of the difference between the two parties. And, given the importance of the issue of ownership both for the foreign investor and host government, the difference between the two parties suggests the extent of the conflict which is likely to develop.

COMPANY POLICIES

Graph 10 presents the distribution of company policies on the extent of ownership in Asia. It should be noted that a company's policy (which represents what a company wants to do) may be quite different from what it actually does or what it can actually get approved from the host government. Therefore, we can interpret company "policy" to mean company "preference."

The single largest category of response, by 37% of the responding companies, is for 100% ownership of Asian investments. However, when local ownership is permitted, the response changes. Thus, of the 32% of the respondents stating majority ownership with minority local owner-ship, 27% prefer such local ownership to be through specific local groups, and only 5% prefer distributing the shares to local nationals. Another 18% of the respondents gave minority ownership with majority local ownership as company policy. However, 14% of these respondents wanted the local ownership to be in the form of specific local groups

GRAPH 10

DISTRIBUTION OF RESPONDENTS' OPINION OF COMPANY POLICY ON EXTENT OF OWNERSHIP OF INVESTMENTS IN ASIA

N=91

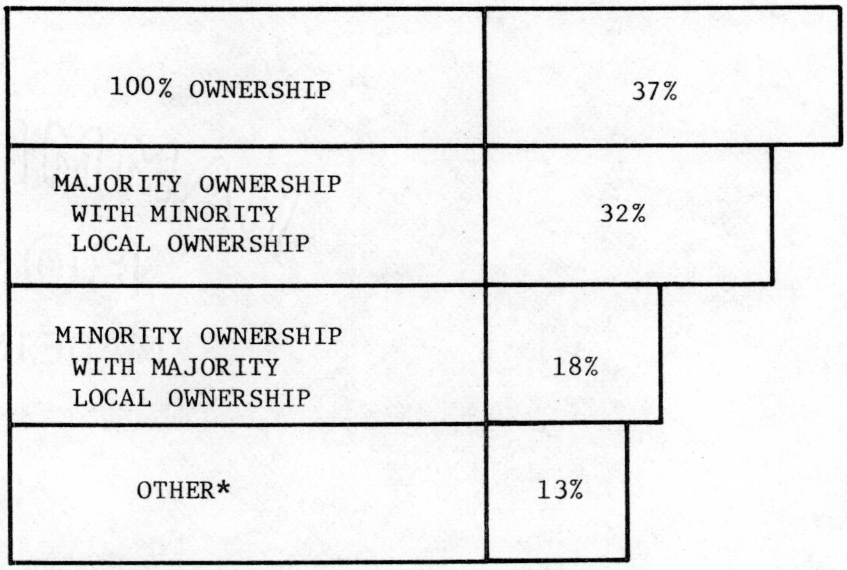

100% OWNERSHIP	37%
MAJORITY OWNERSHIP WITH MINORITY LOCAL OWNERSHIP	32%
MINORITY OWNERSHIP WITH MAJORITY LOCAL OWNERSHIP	18%
OTHER*	13%

*64% HAD NO POLICY
 29% HAD 50/50 OWNERSHIP POLICY
  7% REFERRED TO A WIDE RANGE OF POLICIES

and only 4% sought a wide distribution of local ownership. Therefore, both in cases of majority and minority foreign ownership, it is obvious that responding companies prefer to have specific local groups as co-owners.

Of the remaining 13% of the respondents falling in the "other" category, 64% stated that they had no specific policy but attempted to secure the best arrangement, while 29% stated their policy preference for a 50-50 ownership split with local owners. The remaining responses specified other arrangements.

It is significant that none of the responding companies showed any interest in any of the following choices: initial majority position reduced over time to minority position; majority ownership with host government as minority partner; minority ownership with host government as majority partner. These approaches, however, are being encouraged by Asian governments and promise to be in conflict with the policies and actions of American companies in Asia.

OWNERSHIP CONFIGURATION IN 1971 AND IN FIVE YEARS

The ownership configuration in 1971 reveals the existing arrangements while the configuration in five years reveals the expectations of the responding companies. Graph 11 presents the responses for both time periods.

The largest single category of response for Japan at present is that of minority foreign ownership with majority local ownership. No change is expected in the next five years. A minority foresees no change in the 50-50 ownership split between indigenous and foreign owners in the next five years. However, responding companies expect

53

the Japanese government to permit majority foreign ownership with local ownership. Nevertheless, the Japanese government is expected to become more strict on permitting 100% foreign ownership in the next five years. Therefore, in Japan the major change in five years appears to be a more liberal policy toward majority foreign ownership with minority local ownership.

South Korea is expected to show significant changes on the question of extent of foreign ownership over the next five years. Responding companies expect a significant decline in 100% foreign-owned investment and a dramatic increase in arrangements where the foreign company has minority ownership and local owners hold a majority interest. However, majority foreign ownership with minority local participation will also remain an important type of ownership distribution.

Taiwan will show a dramatic decrease in 100% foreign-owned operations within five years but a significant increase in ownership arrangements where the foreign company retains majority ownership. A significant increase is anticipated in arrangements whereby the foreign company has minority ownership.

The Philippines shows some marked changes on the question of foreign ownership. A dramatic decrease is expected to occur in 100% foreign-ownership arrangements along with an increase in arrangements in which the foreign investor is the minority owner. Responding companies also expect a slight increase in majority foreign ownership with minority local ownership.

As with other developing countries, Indonesia is expected to show a marked decline in 100% foreign-owned operations, a significant growth of arrangements in which the foreign company has majority ownership

with minority local ownership, and a noticeable increase of arrangements in which the foreign company has minority ownership with majority local ownership.

Thailand reveals a less dramatic shift of policies on the extent of foreign ownership. However, 100% foreign ownership is expected to decrease while majority local and minority foreign-ownership arrangements are expected to increase in the next five years.

Malaysia is also expected to impose more restrictions on 100% foreign ownership and significantly to increase arrangements allowing majority ownership with local interests and arrangements in which the foreign company possesses majority equity but with minority local interests.

The prevalent ownership arrangement in India, which is expected to grow dramatically in five years, is minority foreign ownership with majority local interests. Also, 100% foreign ownership will decrease substantially along with a slight increase in arrangements providing the foreign company with majority ownership.

Each Asian country reveals specific characteristics of ownership configuration. In general, however, it is obvious that 100% foreign-owned operations are very much on the decline, and local equity participation will increase in the coming five years. It should be borne in mind that Graph 11 presents the views of responding companies on what they anticipate their ownership configuration will be in five years. Asian governments, on the other hand, might well have a far different attitude on the extent and nature of foreign ownership arrangements they would prefer.

GRAPH 11

DISTRIBUTION OF RESPONDENTS' OPINIONS OF OWNERSHIP
CONFIGURATION OF ASIAN OPERATIONS IN 1971 AND 1976

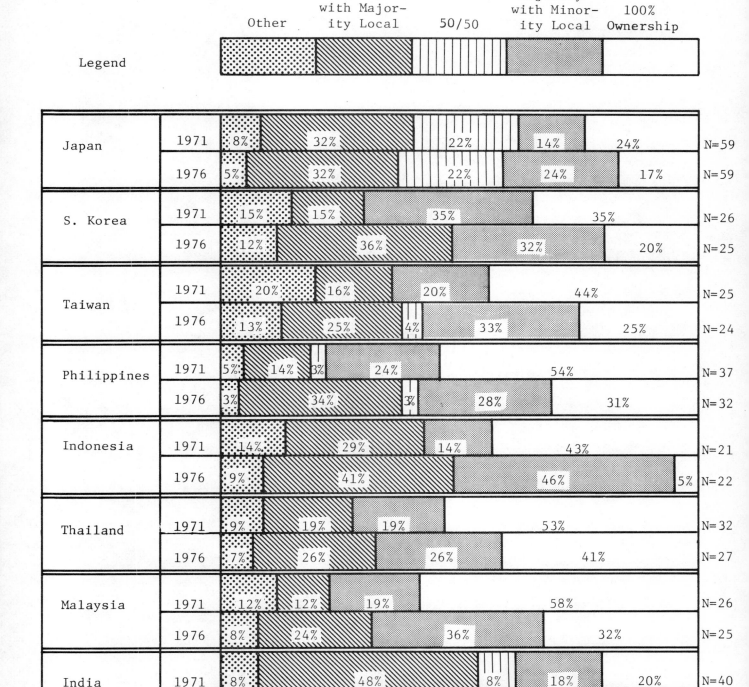

NOTE: PERCENTAGES MAY NOT TOTAL TO 100% BECAUSE OF ROUNDING

56

Graphs 12 and 13 present the distribution of opinions in respect to the attitude of Asian governments on the extent of foreign ownership arrangements in 1971 and in five years. Graph 14 also presents a distribution of the primary reasons for the changes in government attitudes presented in Graph 13. A comparison of the nature of the ownership configuration in Graph 11 with the configuration revealed in Graphs 12 and 13 will offer an idea of the extent of similarity between what responding companies expect to be their ownership configuation in five years versus what they expect to be the policies of host governments in Asia. Differences between the foreign companies and Asian governments on the vital issue of foreign ownership will result in conflict between the two parties.

The reasons for change in government attitudes in five years may be broadly categorized into two areas--those conducive to freedom in extent of foreign ownership and those favoring restrictions on foreign ownership. Thus, the economic growth of a nation creates a growing need for greater foreign resources, and the need for effective participation in international trade and investment calls for a more permissive policy on foreign ownership. A good example of such pressures is Japan. Reduction of a country's foreign exchange problems enables it to be less strict on limiting foreign ownership because the remittance of dividends and royalties in foreign exchange can be provided for by the host country. The opposite situation prevails in countries with foreign exchange limitations requiring a restriction on the extent of foreign ownership in order to lessen the strain on the nation's resources. Thus, a nation's desire to secure managerial skills available from foreign companies will encourage a more open policy toward foreign ownership,

GRAPH 12

DISTRIBUTION OF RESPONDENTS' OPINIONS OF ASIAN GOVERNMENTS'
ATTITUDES IN 1971 TOWARDS EXTENT OF OWNERSHIP OF INVESTMENTS,
LIKE RESPONDENTS

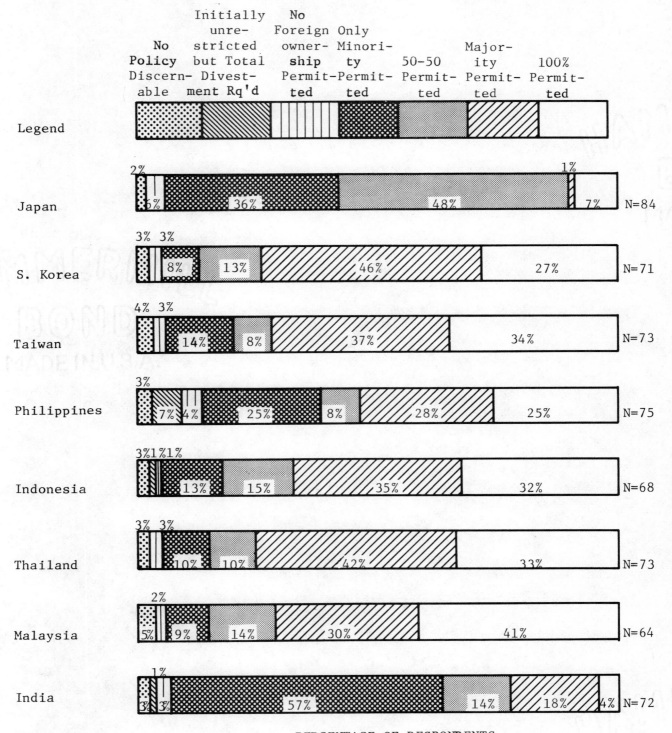

PERCENTAGE OF RESPONDENTS

TOTALS MAY NOT ADD TO 100% BECAUSE OF ROUNDING

GRAPH 13

DISTRIBUTION OF RESPONDENTS' OPINIONS OF ASIAN GOVERNMENTS'
ATTITUDES IN 1976 TOWARDS EXTENT OF OWNERSHIP OF INVESTMENTS,
LIKE RESPONDENTS

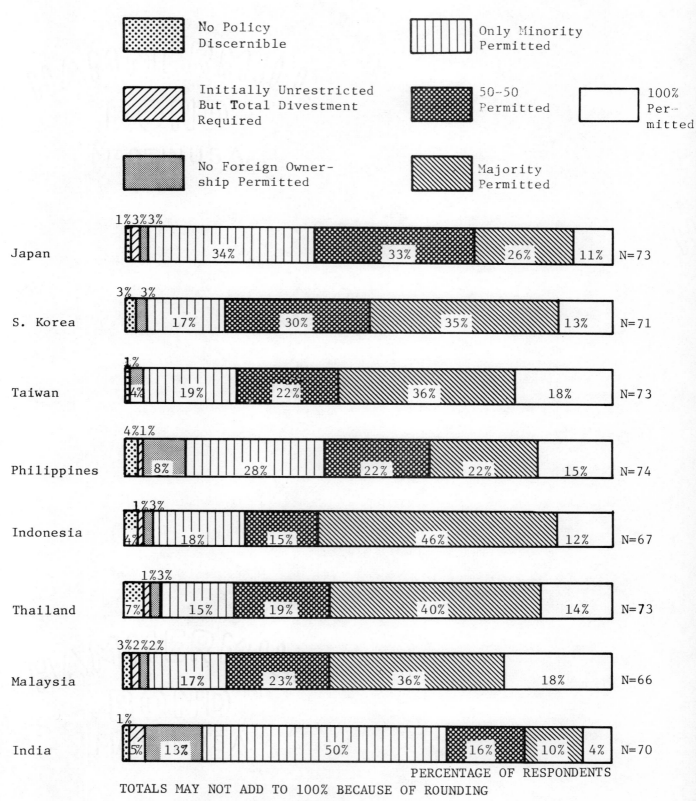

PERCENTAGE OF RESPONDENTS

TOTALS MAY NOT ADD TO 100% BECAUSE OF ROUNDING

59

GRAPH 14

DISTRIBUTION OF RESPONDENTS' PRIMARY REASONS
FOR THEIR OPINIONS OF ASIAN GOVERNMENTS'
ATTITUDES IN 1976 TOWARDS EXTENT OF OWNERSHIP
OF INVESTMENTS

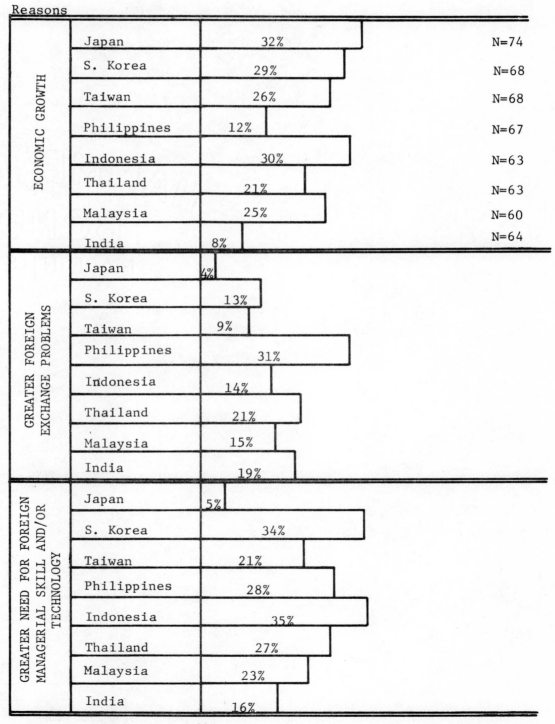

GRAPH 14 (continued)

GREATER PRESSURE BY LOCAL BUSINESSMEN	Japan	34%
	S. Korea	28%
	Taiwan	29%
	Philippines	39%
	Indonesia	21%
	Thailand	35%
	Malaysia	33%
	India	22%
REDUCED FOREIGN EXCHANGE PROBLEMS	Japan	11%
	S. Korea	1%
	Taiwan	3%
	Philippines	1%
	Indonesia	5%
	Thailand	4%
	Malaysia	2%
	India	16%
GREATER ROLE OF GOVERNMENT AS A PARTNER IN INDUSTRIAL PROJECTS	Japan	20%
	S. Korea	16%
	Taiwan	18%
	Philippines	16%
	Indonesia	24%
	Thailand	16%
	Malaysia	17%
	India	55%

GRAPH 14 (continued)

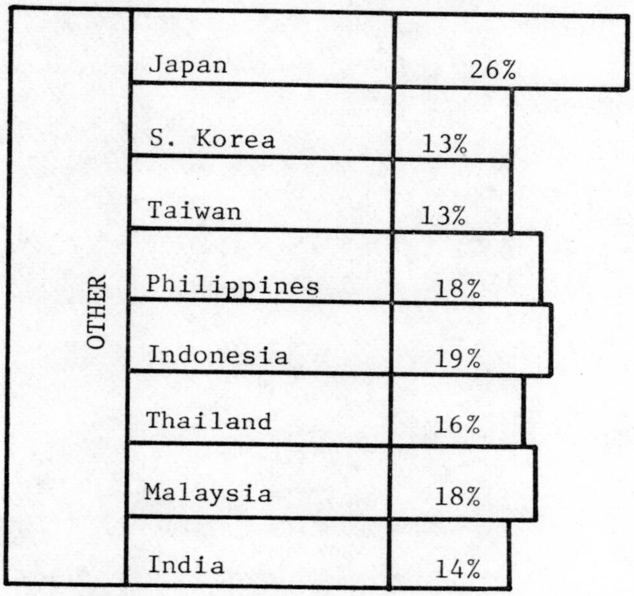

OTHER		
	Japan	26%
	S. Korea	13%
	Taiwan	13%
	Philippines	18%
	Indonesia	19%
	Thailand	16%
	Malaysia	18%
	India	14%

PERCENTAGE OF RESPONDENTS

TOTAL FOR A COUNTRY MAY EXCEED 100% BECAUSE
SOME RESPONDENTS GAVE MORE THAN ONE REASON

especially when such skills might be available only in association with foreign equity interest in local projects.

An interest group of local businessmen may lobby for restrictions on the extent of foreign ownership allowed so that they themselves may profit from the nation's development; on the other hand, where a nation has achieved a high level of economic development (as in the case of Japan) there are likely to be groups seeking liberalization of foreign ownership in order to be able to participate more effectively in international markets. But in the developing countries of Asia, indigenous business interests favor restricting the extent of foreign ownership.

ANALYSIS BY COUNTRY

Japan. Graphs 12 and 13 show that in the coming five years a noticeable decline is expected in Japan in 100%-owned foreign operations and a dramatic increase in arrangements permitting a foreign company to retain majority ownership with local minority ownership. Also, 50-50 ownership split between foreign and Japanese interests is expected to decline in five years. Majority local ownership arrangements are expected to remain a significant aspect of the Japanese economy.

A comparison of Graph 11 with Graphs 12 and 13 shows two major conflict areas in terms of what companies expect their ownership configuration to be in five years and what they expect the Japanese government to seek at that time. The responding companies expect to maintain wholly-owned subsidiaries to a far greater extent than what they expect to be the preference of the Japanese government. Also, companies expect the Japanese government to be seeking 50-50 ownership split arrangements to a greater extent than will be the case in terms of actual corporate policies in five years.

The Japanese government's relaxed attitude toward extent of foreign ownership is seen as the result of economic growth. This term may be variously interpreted. The Japanese will have to permit greater access to foreign companies if Japanese goods and services and foreign direct investment by Japanese companies are to gain favor in overseas markets. In addition, the growing economic importance of Japan in the international economic system will require greater admission of foreign capital and management.

Another reason cited almost as frequently as economic growth is greater pressure by local businessmen. Of course, this point can be a deterrent against liberalization of foreign investments. It also suggests, however, that Japanese companies will be less concerned with large foreign companies as they develop greater confidence in meeting foreign competition, and the Japanese themselves will become more international in their outlook, which will make them less concerned about the extent of foreign ownership or control of Japanese industries than is presently the case.

South Korea. For South Korea, the largest single category of response is majority foreign ownership with minority local interest, followed by 100% foreign ownership and 50-50 ownership split with local interests. However, in five years a significant decline is expected in 100% foreign ownership and majority foreign ownership and a dramatic increase of 50-50 splits and minority foreign ownership.

Comparison of Graphs 12 and 13 with Graph 14 shows that the speed of reduction of 100% foreign ownership will become a conflict issue between foreign companies and the South Korean government. Another conflict

issue with the South Korean government will be on 50-50 ownership split with local interests. The host government will prefer more American investments in this category. The responding companies, however, do not expect their ownership distribution to be in keeping with the government's preferences in five years.

The primary reason why further restrictions on the extent of foreign ownership are not sought is the South Korean government's awareness of the need for foreign managerial and technical skills, followed by the emphasis on economic growth, and to a far lesser extent, the country's deteriorating foreign-exchange position. Respondents mentioned frequently that greater pressure by local businessmen favors increased restrictions on foreign ownership and that the South Korean government will play a greater role in the future as a partner in industrial projects which in turn will result in a reduction in the extent of foreign ownership permitted to foreign companies. For example, the South Korean government is already placing pressure on foreign oil companies to reduce the extent of their ownership by admitting local capital.

Taiwan. Graphs 12 and 13 show that in five years a significant decline of arrangements offering majority ownership to foreign companies and a decline in 100% foreign-owned arrangements is expected in Taiwan. Ownership arrangements providing for a 50-50 split are expected to increase, as are foreign minority ownership arrangements.

As in the case of South Korea, conflict between the government of Taiwan and foreign companies is likely to result over the question of 100% foreign ownership, and the host government is expected to seek 50-50 splits to a greater extent than companies plan to accept.

The government's emphasis on economic growth and the need for foreign managerial and technical skills will encourage it to retain policies attractive to foreign companies. A fewer number of respondents mentioned the country's need for foreign managerial and technical skills as a reason reducing restrictions on the extent of foreign ownership. Taiwan's foreign-exchange problem was not seen as affecting significantly the government's policy on foreign ownership.

As in the case of India and South Korea, greater pressure by local businessmen was most frequently mentioned as the reason for Taiwan's increased restrictions on foreign ownership, followed by a greater role of government as a partner in industrial projects.

The Philippines. The Philippines is expected to show a significant decrease in 100% foreign-owned operations and a dramatic increase in 50-50 arrangements. A significant minority is of the view that the government might restrict foreign investments completely in particular industries and that it might also introduce arrangements whereby the foreign investor divests his ownership interest to local groups over a predetermined period of time.

A comparison with Graph 11 reveals that conflict between foreign investors and the host government is likely to occur in the matter of 100% foreign ownership. In addition, conflicts will develop over 50-50 ownership split arrangements with the government preferring such arrangements to a greater extent than American companies.

The reason mentioned most frequently for a more restrictive policy is greater pressure by local businessmen. In addition, respondents expect the government to play a greater role as a partner in industrial projects.

Greater foreign-exchange problems will also lead to increased restrictions, because government officials are of the opinion that the laissez-faire policy of the past has resulted in unwanted foreign investment causing severe demands on the country's meager foreign exchange reserves. However, respondents frequently mentioned the need for foreign managerial and technical skills, which would tend to reduce the extent of restrictions on foreign ownership.

Indonesia. A significant decline in 100% foreign-owned projects and a growth in majority and minority foreign-owned operations is anticipated for Indonesia. Graph 11 suggests that responding companies anticipate structuring their ownership configuration so as to avoid major conflict areas with the host government.

Indonesia's need for greater foreign managerial skills, followed by economic growth, will reduce pressures for restricting foreign ownership. Respondents believe that the most important reason contributing to a more restrictive policy will be the greater role of the Indonesian government as a partner in projects both in the extractive and manufacturing industries. Local businessmen will also pressure the government for more restrictive policies.

Thailand. The Thai government is expected to reduce greatly the extent of 100% foreign-owned arrangements. Foreign investments with majority foreign ownership will remain the single most important form in five years, but there is likely to be a slight increase of minority foreign-owned projects in Thailand.

A major conflict likely to ensue between the responding companies

and the Thai government will be over the question of the extent and pace of reduction of 100% foreign-owned projects. Graph 11 shows that the responding companies anticipate a far greater number of such arrangements than the Thai government is expected to accept.

Greater pressure on the Thai government by local businessmen, growing foreign exchange problems, and a greater role of the government as a partner in industrial projects will all contribute to a more restrictive policy toward foreign ownership. Restrictions on foreign ownership will lessen as a result of a greater need for foreign managerial and technical skills and a greater stress on economic growth.

Malaysia. Responding companies expect a significant decline in 100% foreign ownership in Malaysia and a noticeable increase in majority foreign-ownership arrangements. They also anticipate an increase of 50-50 split arrangements.

Conflict is expected to result over the matter of 100% ownership, with foreign companies anticipating retaining this form to a greater extent than the Malaysian government is expected to accept.

The government's strongest policies will be tempered by its awareness for greater foreign managerial and technical skills and the stress on economic growth. Pressure by local businessmen will also lead to greater restrictions, and the government will assume a more active role as a partner in industrial projects.

India. India's policy on foreign ownership is the most restrictive of any developing Asian country. The government's policy on 100% foreign ownership will remain the same, namely, very few ownership arrangements

of this type. Minority foreign ownership will remain the predominant type of foreign participation. A significant minority believes that the Indian government will not permit any foreign ownership in certain industries.

Graph 11 shows that responding companies have largely recognized the preferences of the Indian government and anticipate an ownership configuration of their investments in India which is likely to be consistent with the anticipated preferences of the Indian government.

A more restrictive attitude toward foreign ownership is expected to result from the greater role of government as a partner in industrial projects. Because foreign investments are being largely limited to industries which require sizeable local capital participation, the host government is often the only partner with which the foreign company can collaborate. While India possesses large indigenous companies with the capital and managerial resources required for large projects, the government's policy leans clearly toward limiting any future expansion of such companies on grounds that it leads to a concentration of economic power. Therefore, respondents believe that in the coming years they will have to collaborate with the Indian government more frequently. Because the government wishes to have financial control in its hands, foreign companies will be forced to settle for minority equity interest.

REASONS FOR RESTRICTIVE VERSUS NON-RESTRICTIVE POLICIES
One frequently mentioned reason that explains a trend toward a reduction of foreign ownership is greater pressure by local businessmen. Since a greater part of the foreign investments are directed toward meeting

the requirements of the host-country market (i.e., largely or exclusively import substituting), they come into conflict with local business. As a result, local business pressures the government to further restrict the areas and extent of participation in local operations by foreign companies.

On the other hand, reasons which encourage less restrictive policies toward foreign ownership--economic growth, reduced foreign exchange problems, and greater need for foreign managerial skill and/or technology--are also mentioned by respondents, with the greatest weight being placed on the second and third. Governments will be more inclined to approve majority foreign ownership in projects which require exchange for the import of plant and equipment and other essential inputs. But as the foreign-exchange components of the total capitalization of a company dilutes over time, the host government will seek a proportionate or greater reduction of foreign ownership. As new technical and managerial skills are absorbed by the local enterprise, pressures will mount for a reduction of foreign ownership.

SUMMARY: EMERGING TRENDS

The frequency with which responding companies gave similar reasons to explain the tendency of Asian governments to limit the extent of foreign ownership reveals some important trends emerging in Asia. Respondents most frequently referred to greater pressure by local businessmen on their governments to limit the extent of foreign ownership. For a country to attract foreign capital, it must have a liberal policy toward foreign enterprise. However, as soon as the local business community feels that its interests are threatened by the entry of foreign capital,

70

it becomes an important interest group. It appears that foreign investors are already faced with such an interest group, which varies in
size and intensity by country. It is unlikely that the pressure will
be reduced. In the future, therefore, governments will probably seek
more joint ventures, and the foreign company will have to establish a
new pattern of relations with the local partner.

Governments will also play a greater role as partners in industrial
projects. This is due to a lack of local private groups with the resources to undertake major projects. Usually when such groups do exist,
the government limits their expansion. The implication for American
companies is that they will have to learn how to conduct business with
governments as joint-venture partners.

The developing countries of Asia are faced with serious foreign
exchange problems. But, in the opinion of American respondents, host
governments do not view foreign investments as a means of reducing the
foreign exchange gap. Thus, restrictions on the extent of foreign
ownership are only partly motivated, and even then to a small extent by
foreign-exchange considerations. (This observation is supported by
the responses submitted by American companies on types of investments.)

The primary reason why Asian countries encourage foreign investment is that they are aware of their need for managerial and technical
skills and stress the achievement of some minimum targets of economic
growth.

4

Types of Investment

The foreign investment climate of a country is strongly affected by
the types of investments encouraged or permitted by the government.
Some of the main types of investment are: manufacture largely for
export, manufacture largely for the host-country market, extractive
industries, management services contracts, technology-intensive investments, and labor-intensive investments. These types of investments
are often interrelated. For example, manufacture for exports may
require a technology-intensive investment, as in the case of integrated circuits. Or it can also include labor-intensive investments
such as the assembly of parts and components of electronic products.

The preferences of companies and of governments toward a particular kind of investment can also vary significantly, and such differences determine the type of investment which a company may be permitted
to make. Some of the determinants of a company's policy toward types
of foreign investments are: overall corporate policy (e.g., manufacturing for exports will be undertaken only in countries permitting 100%-
owned subsidiaries); allocation of corporate expenditure of resources
on a worldwide basis; the size of the host-country market; risks
inherent in a market; and the precedent setting effect of an investment
(resulting in other countries seeking similar investments). However,
a government's preference for a particular type of investment may be

in conflict with a foreign investor's preference.

This chapter presents the attitudes expected of Asian governments toward the different types of investments. The configuration of investments by type (analyzed above in Graph 5) and the expected configuration over the next five years are also presented. A comparison of Graph 5 and Graphs 15 and 16 reveals the potential conflict areas between host governments in Asia and the foreign investor on types of investments.

MANUFACTURE LARGELY FOR EXPORTS

Foreign-exchange limitations are already a major limitation for many Asian countries who wish to carry on their development plans. Asian governments are beginning to recognize the need for foreign investment largely for export purposes. Graphs 15 and 16 present the distribution of response of attitudes of Asian governments in 1971 and in five years thereafter toward foreign direct investment for the purpose of manufacturing largely for exports. Graph 5 presents the existing distribution of types of investments in Asia by the responding companies, including the extent to which foreign companies manufacture in Asia largely for exports.

Graph 5 shows that American companies do not undertake manufacturing operations in Japan largely for export purposes because of the higher cost of labor, restrictions on extent of foreign ownership, and the relatively lower comparative advantage of Japanese manufacturing operations versus other Asian countries in relatively low-level technology or labor-intensive industries.

Graphs 15 and 16 reveal that responding companies expect the

73

GRAPH 15

DISTRIBUTION OF RESPONDENTS' OPINIONS OF ASIAN GOVERNMENTS' ATTITUDES IN 1971 TOWARDS FOREIGN DIRECT INVESTMENT FOR THE PURPOSE OF MANUFACTURING LARGELY FOR EXPORT

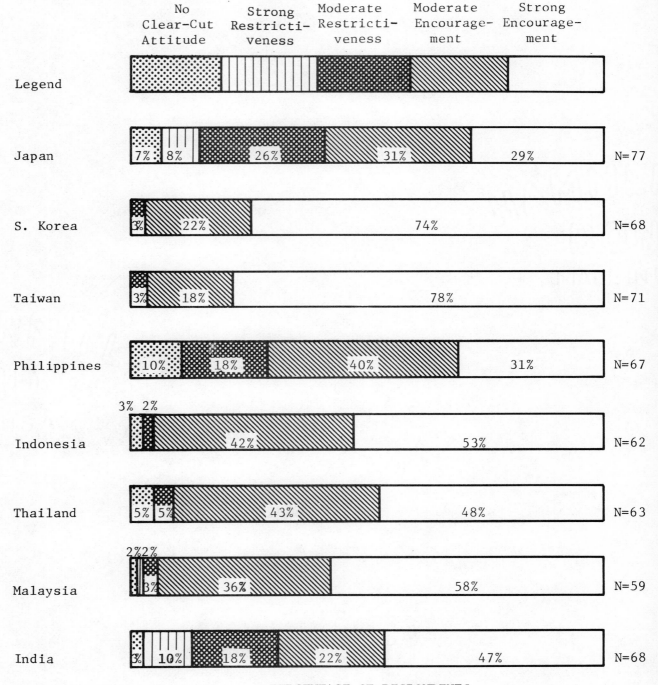

PERCENTAGE OF RESPONDENTS

TOTALS MAY NOT ADD TO 100% BECAUSE OF ROUNDING

74

GRAPH 16

DISTRIBUTION OF RESPONDENTS' OPINIONS OF ASIAN
GOVERNMENTS' ATTITUDES IN 1976 TOWARDS FOREIGN
DIRECT INVESTMENT FOR THE PURPOSE OF MANUFACTURING
LARGELY FOR EXPORT

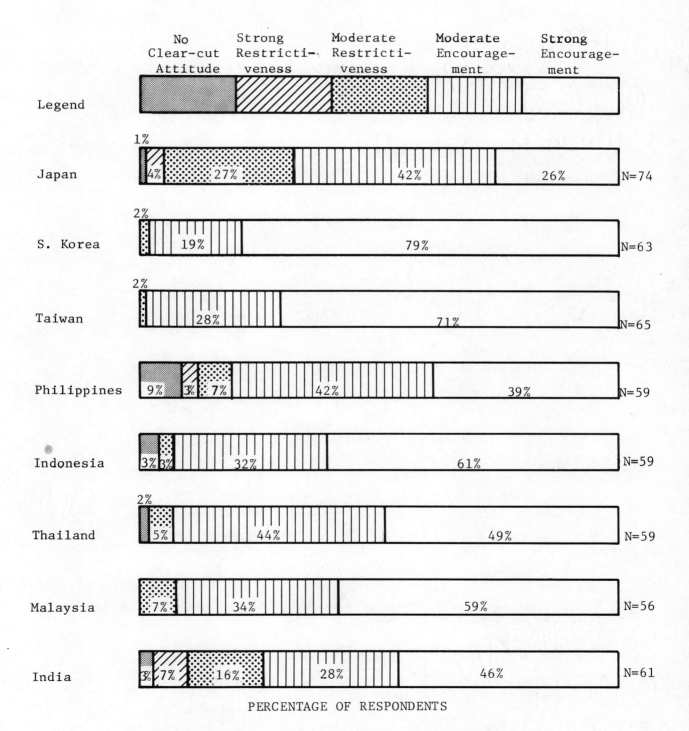

PERCENTAGE OF RESPONDENTS

TOTALS MAY NOT ADD TO 100% BECAUSE OF ROUNDING

Japanese government to place greater stress on manufacturing largely for export than is revealed in Graph 5. The Japanese government is placed at present under the categories of moderate encouragement and strong encouragement. It is not expected to change significantly in five years.

The difference between the existing distribution of types of foreign investments and the expected attitudes of governments in the developing countries of Asia is significant; the potential for conflict on this point is therefore considerable.

As seen in the comparison of Graph 5 with Graphs 15 and 16, South Korea shows a major gap. The South Korean government strongly encourages manufacturing largely for exports; this trend will grow in the next five years. The extent of the existing use of South Korea for export purposes by American companies versus preferences of the host government takes on added significance when it is recognized that South Korea has been one of the few Asian countries which has achieved some success in exporting goods manufactured by foreign investors.

The response for Taiwan is similar to that for South Korea. The Taiwan government is expected to offer strong encouragement to manufacturing largely for exports both at present and in five years. Yet, as revealed in Graph 5, responding companies place far less emphasis on this type of operation than they expect the host government to require of them. (The relatively greater uncertainty characterizing Taiwan at present, as a result of Mainland China's admission to the United Nations and U.S. policies toward Taiwan, is likely to change the American investor's view of Taiwan as a significant manufacturing base catering to the worldwide or regional market needs of the organization.)

Responding companies expect the Filipino government to offer moderate to strong encouragement, both at present and in five years, to foreign investors in manufacturing largely for export. As shown in Graph 5, however, the existing distribution of American investments reveals only a minuscule effort by American companies in that direction. Given the worsening foreign exchange position of the Philippines, it is more than likely that the Filipino government will place far greater emphasis on requiring exports both by indigenous and foreign companies.

The general trend shown by the other developing countries of Asia also applies to Indonesia. Respondents expect the government to place growing emphasis on foreign manufacturing largely for export both at present and in five years. This emphasis is in sharp contrast to the existing use of Indonesia as a manufactuing base for export purposes. The same holds true for Thailand, Malaysia, and India.

MANUFACTURE FOR HOST-COUNTRY MARKET

Developing countries have sought foreign investments primarily to encourage the development of local industry, which results in some self-sufficiency while also saving in foreign exchange through displacement of imports.

The policies of countries shift over time in terms of the particular product lines they seek from foreign investors. For example, while Indonesia seeks foreign investments in the manufacture of simple machine tools, India does not seek this type of investment because of the relatively advanced level of indigenous technology. Policies on types of investment also vary by the relative priorities of the economic plans. For several years, many Asian countries encouraged

the establishment of prestige industries (steel mills, petrochemical plants, etc.) while largely ignoring investments that would raise their agriculture output. In the recent past, however, many Asian countries have emphasized the improvement of agriculture.

Graphs 17 and 18 present the views on the attitude of Asian governments toward foreign investments in manufacturing which are designed primarily to cater to the host-country market. Graph 5 shows the existing country distribution of this type of investment.

The Japanese government is presently restrictive toward foreign investments for purposes of manufacturing largely for the host-country market. The largest single category of response is that of strong restrictiveness, followed by moderate restrictiveness. No significant shift is expected in five years, especially in terms of a dramatic opening up of the Japanese economy to foreign investments which are designed largely for catering to the Japanese market.

Unlike Japan, the developing countries of Asia in general encourage manufacturing operations that cater largely to the host-country market. Both South Korea and Taiwan show an encouraging attitude at present but will be changing toward a more restrictive attitude in five years. The same general characteristic holds true for the Philippines.

Indonesia at present is viewed as encouraging such investments, and this attitude is likely to remain over the next five years. However, a slight increase in the existing level of restrictiveness of foreign investments in manufacturing is expected. The configuration of responses for Thailand and Malaysia at present and in five years corresponds closely to that of Indonesia.

GRAPH 17

DISTRIBUTION OF RESPONDENTS' OPINIONS OF ASIAN GOVERNMENTS' ATTITUDES IN 1971 TOWARDS FOREIGN DIRECT INVESTMENT FOR THE PURPOSE OF MANUFACTURING LARGELY FOR THE HOST-COUNTRY MARKET

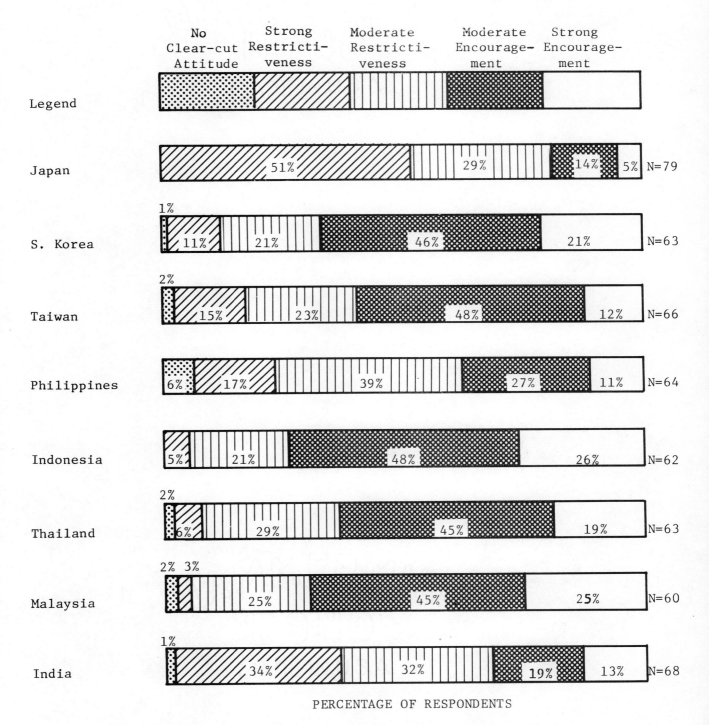

PERCENTAGE OF RESPONDENTS

TOTALS MAY NOT ADD TO 100% BECAUSE OF ROUNDING

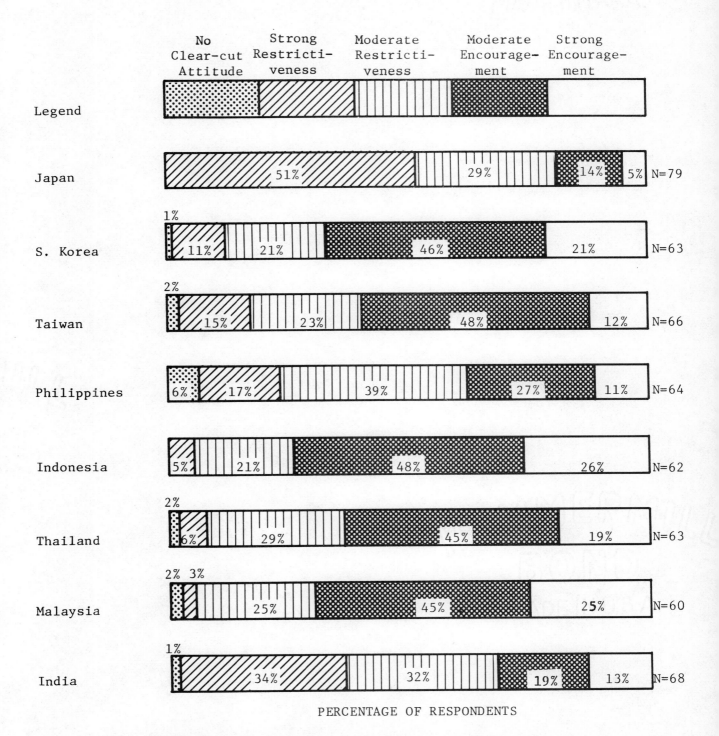

GRAPH 17

DISTRIBUTION OF RESPONDENTS' OPINIONS OF ASIAN
GOVERNMENTS' ATTITUDES IN 1971   TOWARDS FOREIGN
DIRECT INVESTMENT FOR THE PURPOSE OF MANUFACTURING
LARGELY FOR THE HOST-COUNTRY MARKET

PERCENTAGE OF RESPONDENTS

TOTALS MAY NOT ADD TO 100% BECAUSE OF ROUNDING

GRAPH 18

DISTRIBUTION OF RESPONDENTS' OPINIONS OF ASIAN GOVERNMENTS' ATTITUDES IN 1976 TOWARDS FOREIGN DIRECT INVESTMENT FOR THE PURPOSE OF MANUFACTURING LARGELY FOR HOST-COUNTRY MARKET

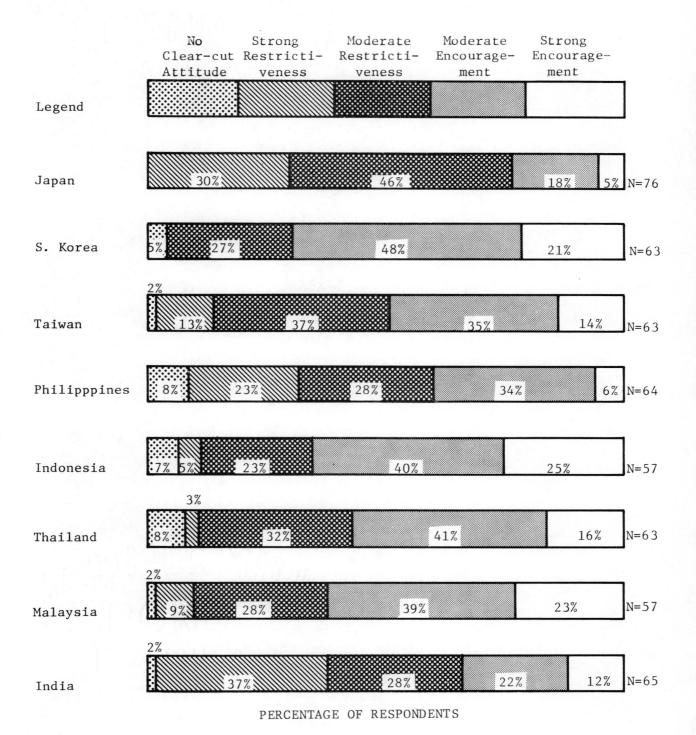

PERCENTAGE OF RESPONDENTS

TOTALS MAY NOT ADD TO 100% BECAUSE OF ROUNDING

The largest response for India falls under the category of strong restrictiveness, followed by moderate restrictiveness. It is not expected to change in the next five years.

MANAGEMENT SERVICES CONTRACTS

Management services contracts reveal a wide range of combinations. They may or may not involve an equity interest in the project to be managed. Both types are considered in this response.

Graph 5 shows that management services contracts account for only a limited number of the various types of operations of American companies in Asia, and the response in Graphs 19 and 20 reveals the attitudes of Asian governments.

Japan is considered a restrictive country, which is not likely to change in the next five years, although there will be a slight shift toward a more encouraging attitude. The developing countries of Asia reveal varying characteristics.

Responding companies interpret the existing attitude of the South Korean government to be generally encouraging toward management services contracts, and the same attitude is likely to persist over the next five years. However, a significant percentage of the responding companies expect a growth in restrictiveness as well: for example, Taiwan and the Philippines.

Indonesia reveals a different tendency. It is expected to remain favorable toward management services contracts. Thailand and Malaysia reveal an attitude at present and in five years which is similar to the one for Indonesia. India, on the other hand, is expected to be generally restrictive in five years as it is at present.

GRAPH 19

DISTRIBUTION OF RESPONDENTS' OPINIONS OF ASIAN
GOVERNMENTS' ATTITUDES IN 1971 TOWARDS FOREIGN
MANAGEMENT SERVICES CONTRACTS

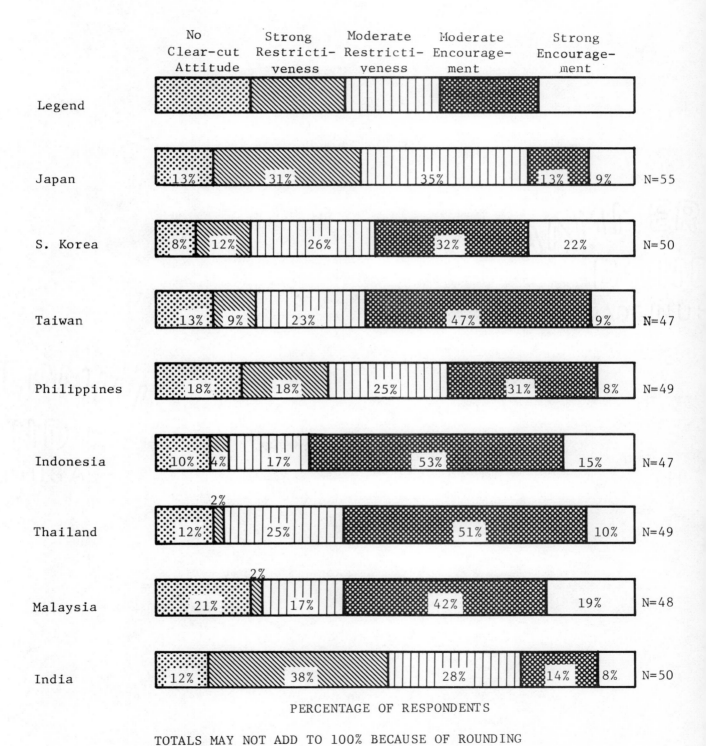

PERCENTAGE OF RESPONDENTS

TOTALS MAY NOT ADD TO 100% BECAUSE OF ROUNDING

GRAPH 20

DISTRIBUTION OF RESPONDENTS' OPINIONS OF ASIAN
GOVERNMENTS' ATTITUDES IN 1976 TOWARDS FOREIGN
MANAGEMENT SERVICES CONTRACTS

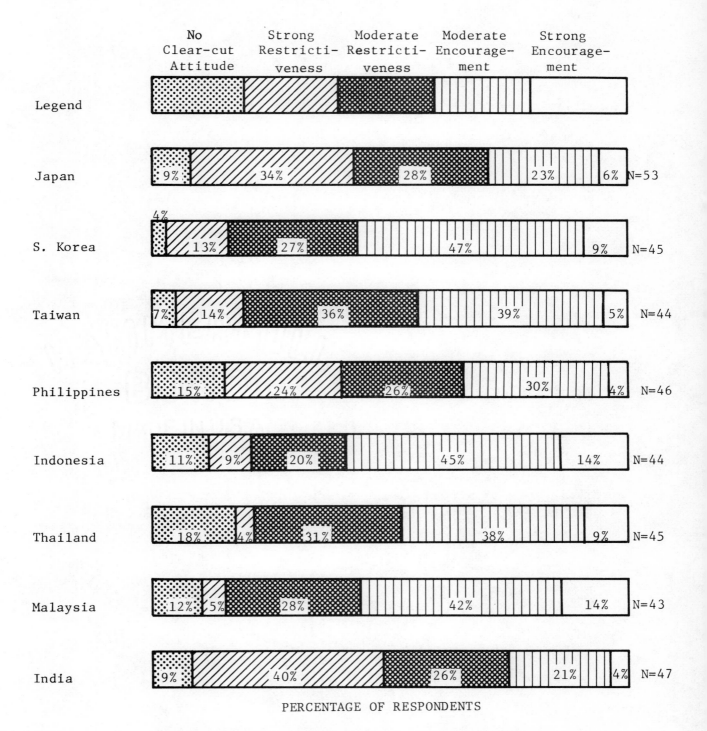

PERCENTAGE OF RESPONDENTS

TOTALS MAY NOT ADD TO 100% BECAUSE OF ROUNDING

In general, the country-by-country analysis suggests that the majority of Asian countries will become more restrictive toward management services contracts with foreign companies.

TECHNOLOGY-INTENSIVE INVESTMENTS

Developing countries seek the technology and know-how possessed by foreign companies. Japan has preferrred licensing agreements or outright acquisition of technology from foreign sources rather than permitting foreigners to own Japanese companies. While Asian countries seek technology-intensive investments, the levels of indigenous technology and the capacity of countries to absorb foreign technology vary considerably. India is technologically more advanced than Malaysia or Indonesia, and in several cases Indian companies have sold technology to other Asian countries. Therefore, the question on host government attitudes toward technology-intensive investments should be interpreted to mean the level of technology which the recipient countries would consider to be "intensive" even though such levels might be viewed as less than intensive in the context of other countries.

Graphs 21 and 22 present the views of responding companies. It should be pointed out, first, that it is a matter of pride for a country to have technology-intensive industries. Second, some technology-intensive industries hold the promise of exports, and therefore, not only help bring in foreign exchange but also diversify a country's export base by including an increasing range of manufactured goods. The export of technology-intensive products from developing countries also greatly enhances a country's image abroad. Third, in some Asian countries, both government and business are seeking ever more complex technologies, in

GRAPH 21

DISTRIBUTION OF RESPONDENTS' OPINIONS OF ASIAN
GOVERNMENTS' ATTITUDES IN 1971 TOWARDS FOREIGN
TECHNOLOGY-INTENSIVE INVESTMENTS

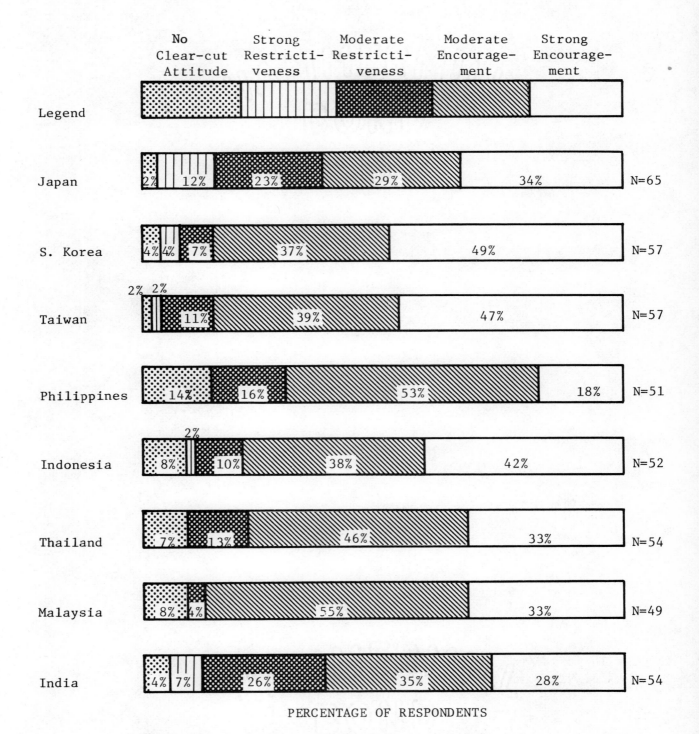

PERCENTAGE OF RESPONDENTS

TOTALS MAY NOT ADD TO 100% BECAUSE OF ROUNDING

GRAPH 22

DISTRIBUTION OF RESPONDENTS' OPINIONS OF ASIAN
GOVERNMENTS' ATTITUDES IN 1976 TOWARDS FOREIGN
TECHNOLOGY-INTENSIVE INVESTMENTS

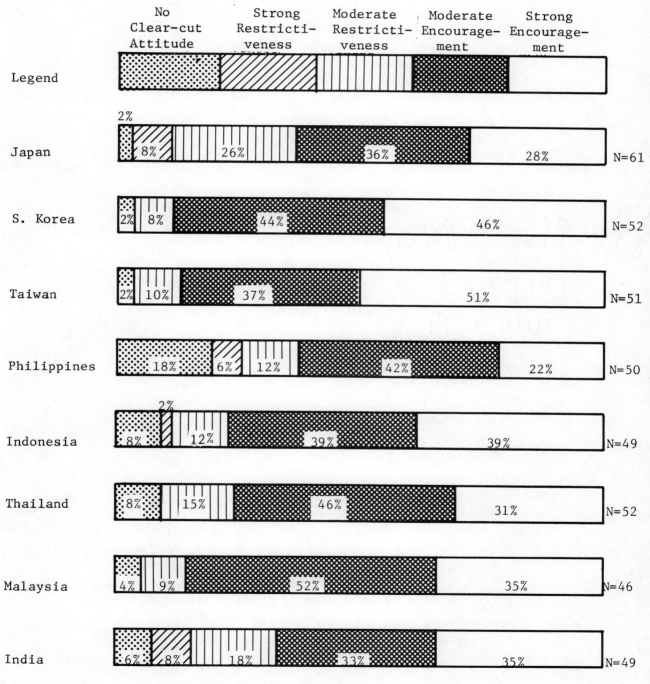

PERCENTAGE OF RESPONDENTS

TOTALS MAY NOT ADD TO 100% BECAUSE OF ROUNDING

the belief that they are qualified to cope with them. The foreign investor will be required to offer increasingly advanced technologies often at a pace determined by the host government. Japan and the developing countries of Asia encourage technology-intensive investments, and the situation is not expected to change in the next five years. Although India is favorably inclined toward such investments, its policies are quite restrictive. The essential question is whether the Asian countries can offer terms and conditions under which foreign investors will make such investments.

LABOR-INTENSIVE INVESTMENTS

A characteristic common to all Asian countries, with the exception of Japan, is the high levels of unemployment and underemployment. Low literacy levels and lack of an industrial tradition make it difficult for some Asian workers to master advanced types of machines or other forms of technology. For example, certain kinds of equipment require continuous service and maintenance, but Asian workers are not prepared for such rigid standards. Asian governments are faced with the serious task of finding employment and a profession for their citizens, and technology-intensive equipment such as computers or even tractors displace far too many workers. For these and other reasons, Asian governments often seek labor-intensive investments by foreign companies.

Graph 23 and 24 show the attitudes of Asian governments toward foreign investments in labor-intensive projects.

Japan differs from the other Asian countries in that its present policy of moderate restrictiveness is not expected to change in five years. However, Japan is faced with the problem of a highly industrialized country: rising wages and serious shortages of workers—a situation not found in

GRAPH 23

DISTRIBUTION OF RESPONDENTS' OPINIONS OF ASIAN GOVERNMENTS' ATTITUDES IN 1971 TOWARDS FOREIGN LABOR-INTENSIVE INVESTMENTS

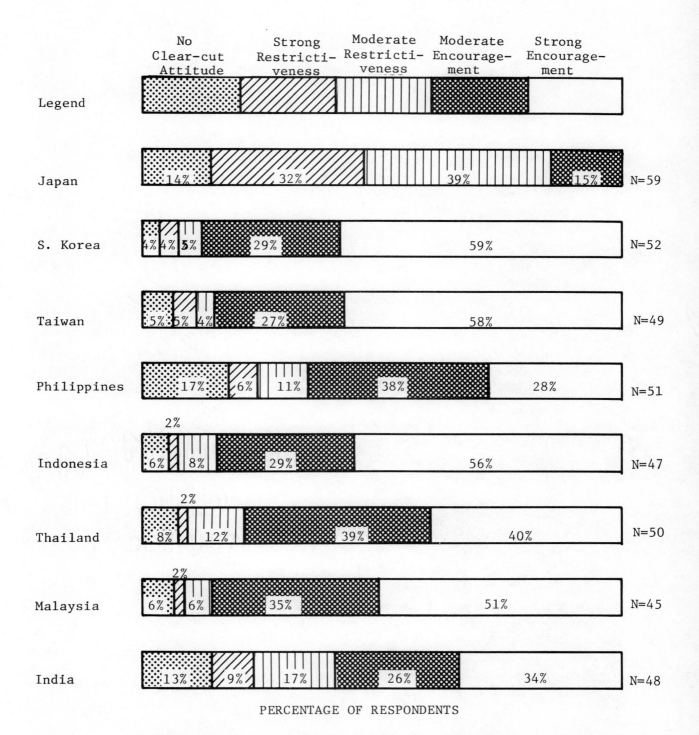

PERCENTAGE OF RESPONDENTS

TOTALS MAY NOT ADD TO 100% BECAUSE OF ROUNDING

GRAPH 24

DISTRIBUTION OF RESPONDENTS' OPINIONS OF ASIAN GOVERNMENTS' ATTITUDES IN 1976 TOWARDS FOREIGN LABOR-INTENSIVE INVESTMENTS

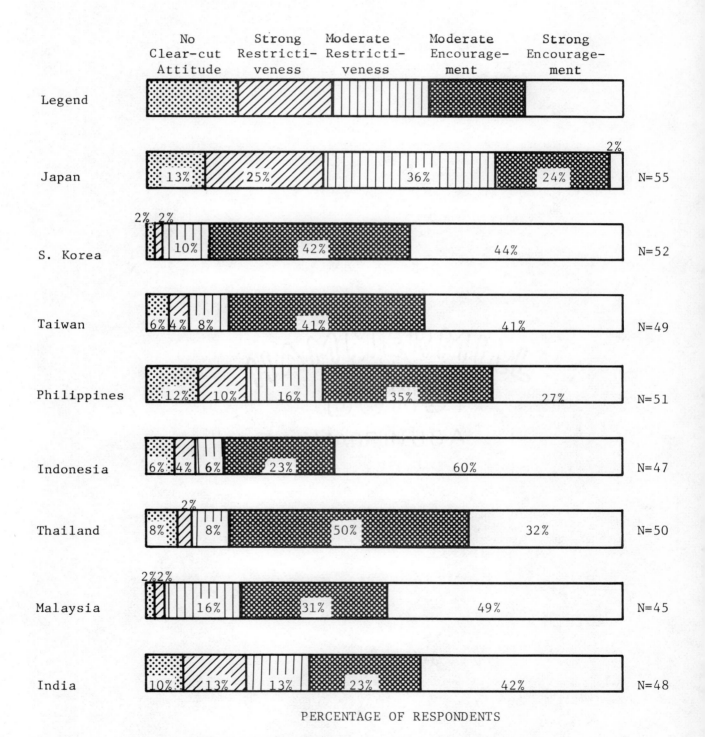

PERCENTAGE OF RESPONDENTS

TOTALS MAY NOT ADD TO 100% BECAUSE OF ROUNDING

other Asian countries. All the developing countries of Asia show
moderate encouragement toward labor-intensive investments. In fact,
South Korea, Taiwan, and Indonesia lean toward the strong encouragement category at present and in five years, while Thailand and Malaysia
are solidly in the moderate encouragement category, as are India and
the Philippines, the latter two revealing a slight inclination toward
the category of no clear-cut policy.

5

OPERATING PROBLEMS

The objective of this chapter is to explore the problems arising in everyday operations from the restrictions imposed by a host government on foreign business, such as: use of expatriate personnel; increasing local content requirements; currency instability; earnings remittance policy; host government price controls; import restrictions; and time for project approval.

EXPATRIATE PERSONNEL

All countries place some form of restriction on the employment of foreign nationals in local operations, and several Asian countries have exerted strong pressures for the employment of nationals, particularly at the lower and intermediate levels of the organization. Foreign companies also encourage the employment of nationals because it is less expensive than relocating personnel from the United States.

Because senior management levels require a period of training-- business "know-how" is often the result of long experience--companies seldom entrust sizeable operations to a person whose primary qualification is his nationality. But when a host government demands the employment of nationals at senior levels of management, companies begin to worry.

The following sections discuss the extent of the pressure upon foreign companies operating in Asia to employ nationals at the most senior levels of management, and it also shows the managerial positions a company usually first assigns to nationals.

Extent of Pressure. Graph 25 offers a distribution of the extent of pressure, if any, exerted by host governments on the employment of nationals at senior management levels.

India is quite restrictive in this respect. The category mentioned most frequently by respondents is strong pressure with a fixed deadline of within five years, followed by moderate pressure with deadline within five years.

With respect to Japan, the majority of the respondents felt that there was either no pressure or only slight pressure for the employment of nationals, but without a time limit for withdrawal of expatriates. The next most frequently mentioned category was strong pressure with a fixed deadline of within five years. Thus, the Japanese situation, in the view of the respondents, is characterized by somewhat extreme situations--either limited if any pressure or strong pressure.

The greatest frequency of response for the Philippines was for the category of slight pressure, but no deadline, followed by no pressure and moderate pressure with deadline of over five years. A minority referred to indigenization of senior management positions within five years or less.

The largest single category of response for South Korea was no pressure, followed by slight pressure, but no deadline. However, a significant minority mentioned moderate or strong pressures for the employment of nationals.

92

GRAPH 25

DISTRIBUTION OF RESPONDENTS' OPINIONS OF THE
PRESSURE OF ASIAN GOVERNMENTS TO USE NATIONALS
AT SENIOR MANAGEMENT LEVELS

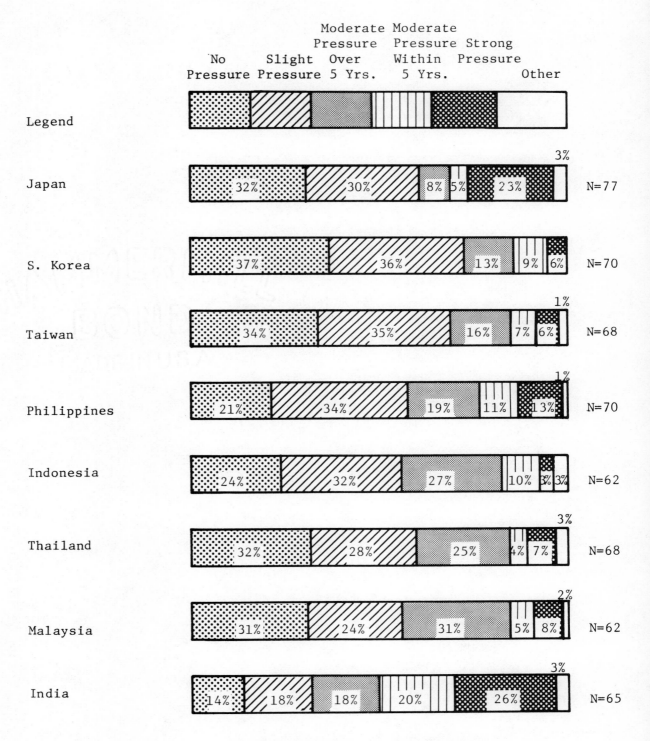

PERCENTAGE OF RESPONDENTS

TOTAL MAY NOT ADD TO 100% BECAUSE OF ROUNDING

The pattern for Taiwan is similar to that of South Korea.

According to a majority of the responding companies, the Indonesian government has either exerted no pressure or only slight pressure. A significant minority, however, has referred to varying degrees of pressure.

The pattern for Thailand and Malaysia is basically similar to that of Indonesia.

On the whole, Asian governments presently do not interfere with the employment practices of foreign companies as these relate to senior management levels. Nevertheless, this overall response must be viewed in relation to the response for other categories (such as extent of foreign ownership) which shows a clear tendency toward a more restrictive policy on foreign investments. Therefore, one can expect Asian governments to speed up the pace of indigenization of senior management levels within the next five years.

Levels of Indigenization. Different managerial areas have changing levels of importance for a company, depending on the stage of project development, characteristics of the local market, nature of the product line, and extent of pressure by the host government and local partner. These areas which a company will assign to nationals indicates what areas executives believe nationals are equipped to handle. It also suggests the areas which foreign companies feel are most likely to be the first ones to be challenged by the host government or local partners and therefore the ones where foreign companies would make a special effort to cultivate the skills of nationals.

Respondents were asked to indicate the order in which they would with-

draw expatriates in favor of nationals in their Asian operations, in the following positions: namely, president, financial manager, plant production and/or technical manager, and marketing manager. Graph 26 shows the response.

In general, the office of president is the last position responding companies would turn over to a national. Naturally, this position has the greatest influence on the development of local operations and is closest to the parent company. Retaining an expatriate as president is more important when the foreign company has significant majority ownership or a wholly-owned subsidiary than in cases in which the foreign company has a minority interest.

A significant minority of the respondents, nevertheless, ranked the position of president as the first or the second position they would indigenize. This response would apply to companies with minority ownership or those in which the local partner possesses expertise of undisputed quality.

The position of financial manager is usually the next-to-last position to be indigenized. Unlike the post of president there is a more even distribution of responses in this category. A significant minority ranked this as the fourth and fifth positions to be indigenized. However, a slightly higher percentage, but still a minority, listed it as the first or second position to be indigenized. The explanation is that foreign companies are less inclined to keep this function in the hands of expatriates, and companies with majority ownership or wholly-owned subsidiaries are disinclined to indigenize this function too rapidly on the grounds that the systems for controlling the operations are often based on financial controls. Financial policies of the parent (such as

GRAPH 26

DISTRIBUTION OF RESPONDENTS' ESTIMATE OF RELATIVE WITHDRAWAL OF TOP EXPATRIATE MANAGEMENT PERSONNEL FROM THEIR OVERSEAS OPERATIONS

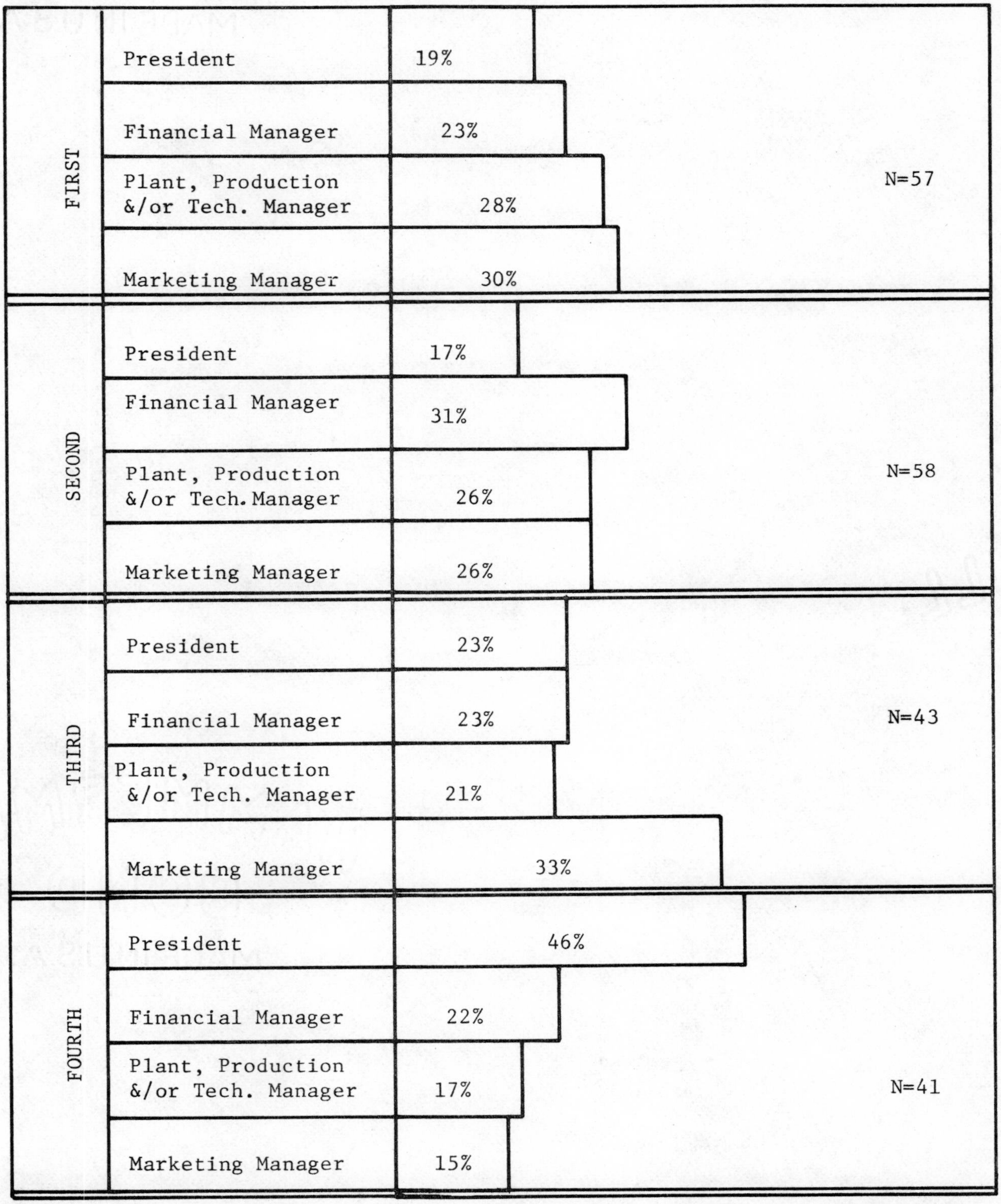

FIRST

President	19%
Financial Manager	23%
Plant, Production &/or Tech. Manager	28%
Marketing Manager	30%

N=57

SECOND

President	17%
Financial Manager	31%
Plant, Production &/or Tech. Manager	26%
Marketing Manager	26%

N=58

THIRD

President	23%
Financial Manager	23%
Plant, Production &/or Tech. Manager	21%
Marketing Manager	33%

N=43

FOURTH

President	46%
Financial Manager	22%
Plant, Production &/or Tech. Manager	17%
Marketing Manager	15%

N=41

decisions on dividends and intra-corporate transfer pricing) are often
sensitive areas which companies prefer to keep in the hands of trusted
expatriates until such time that a national has become sufficiently
a "company man."

In joint ventures, especially those in which the host-government has
a significant minority interest, the U.S. company often insists on naming
an expatriate as financial manager, in order to retain some financial
control over the critical areas of local operations.

The positions of plant/production/technical manager and the marketing
manager were next to be indigenized. A majority of the respondents
ranked the plant manager's function as the first or second to be indigenized. However, a significant minority placed it among the last and next-
to-last functions to be indigenized. The preference of a company depends
on the technical sophistication of a product, the size of the project,
and the extent to which trained nationals are available.

As with the position of plant production manager, a majority of the
respondents placed the marketing manager's position as the first or second
to be indigenized. But a significant minority placed it as the fourth
position to be indigenized, with a far smaller percentage placing it last.
The tendency toward a relatively rapid indigenization of the marketing
function is due to several reasons. Marketing requires interaction and
intimate understanding of the local social-cultural factors. And, given
the significant social-cultural-economic differences between Asian countries
and the United States or Western Europe, a national often is best suited
for a position in marketing. In addition, many Asian countries are
sellers' markets, which reduces the importance of the marketing function.
American companies are often particularly short of skilled senior-level

marketing personnel, whom they prefer to assign to the highly competitive markets of Western Europe where the companies usually maintain far larger operations.

The order of indigenization of senior management sheds some light on the characteristics of American companies operating in Asia. For many, a critical consideration is to manage the overall country level operations in a way which permits effective integration with the company's world-wide operations. But respondents are also aware of the need for nationals, especially in cases in which a national would be at an advantage in terms of interacting with the local environment which a Westerner is unlikely to fully comprehend.

INCREASING LOCAL CONTENT REQUIREMENTS

Governments often encourage or force companies to use an ever-larger percentage of local material and services in their products. For example, when a new type of operation is first established, a government might permit 50% or more in terms of imported content. But thereafter the government may insist that an ever-larger percentage be of local origin as a way of saving foreign exchange and developing local industries. Difficulties arise when the local content is simply not available, is of inferior quality, or is supposed to be available but the suppliers are unable to deliver the goods.

Graphs 27 and 28 show the distribution of responses. India is conflictive on this point, with a majority of the respondents stating major and severely handicapping difficulties. In the next five years, a significant increase is expected in the severely handicapping category.

In the other seven Asian countries, the overwhelming percentage of

GRAPH 27

DISTRIBUTION OF RESPONDENTS' OPINIONS OF
LEVEL OF DIFFICULTY CAUSED BY ASIAN GOVERNMENTS'
DEMAND FOR INCREASING LOCAL CONTENT
REQUIREMENTS IN 1971

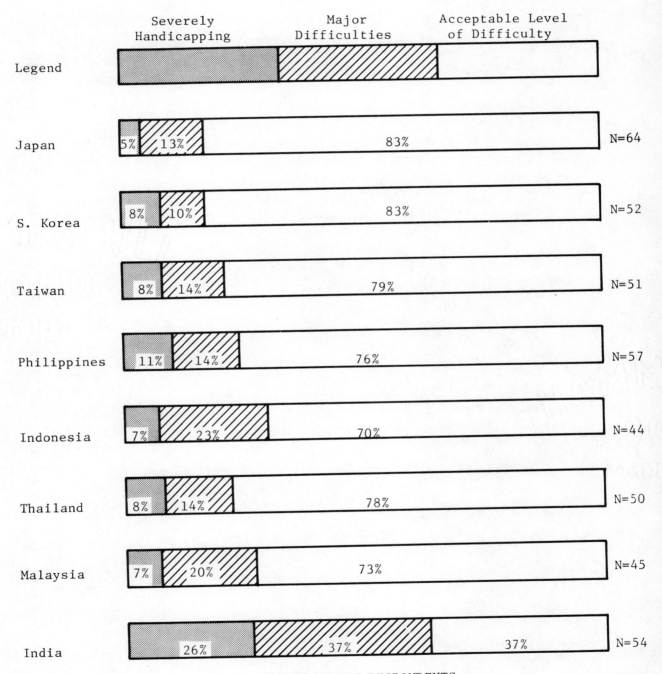

PERCENTAGE OF RESPONDENTS

TOTALS MAY NOT ADD TO 100% BECAUSE OF ROUNDING

GRAPH 28

DISTRIBUTION OF RESPONDENTS' OPINIONS OF THE
EXPECTED LEVEL OF DIFFICULTY TO BE CAUSED BY
ASIAN GOVERNMENTS' DEMANDS FOR INCREASING
LOCAL CONTENT REQUIREMENTS IN 1976

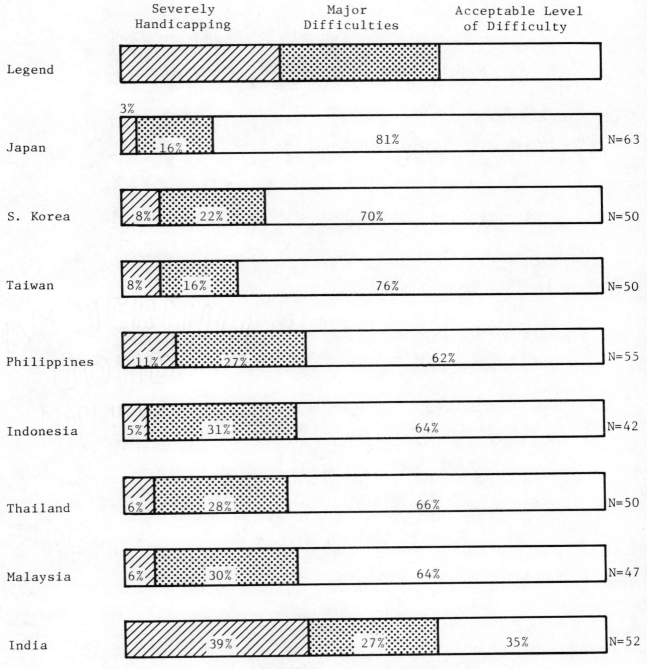

PERCENTAGE OF RESPONDENTS

TOTALS MAY NOT ADD TO 100% BECAUSE OF ROUNDING

the respondents consider the host governments' demand for increasing local content requirement to be at an acceptable level of difficulty at present. In five years, however, respondents expect it to present major difficulties.

CURRENCY INSTABILITY

With the exception of Japan, most Asian countries are faced with balance of payments and balance of trade problems. Devaluations have occurred and will occur in the future. Graphs 29 and 30 show the responses to the level of difficulty in operations due to currency instability in various Asian countries.

The Philippines presents the greatest difficulty both at present and in five years. A large majority consider currency instability in the Philippines to be a source of major problems at present and in five years. India's currency problems are serious now and are expected to worsen in the coming five years. Japan's currency situation, on the other hand, is rather stable and it is expected to remain so in the next five years.

The other Asian countries fall somewhere between India and Japan in terms of the level of operational difficulties caused by currency instability: South Korea's currency instability is at an acceptable level presently, but it is expected to worsen within the next five years. A minority see the South Korean situation as being major and severely handicapping at present and in five years. Indonesia is viewed as presenting major and severely handicapping problems for a majority of the respondents at present and in five years. The majority of the respondents consider Thailand's currency instability to be at an acceptable level at

GRAPH 29

DISTRIBUTION OF RESPONDENTS' OPINIONS OF LEVEL
OF DIFFICULTY CAUSED BY ASIAN GOVERNMENTS'
CURRENCY INSTABILITY IN 1971

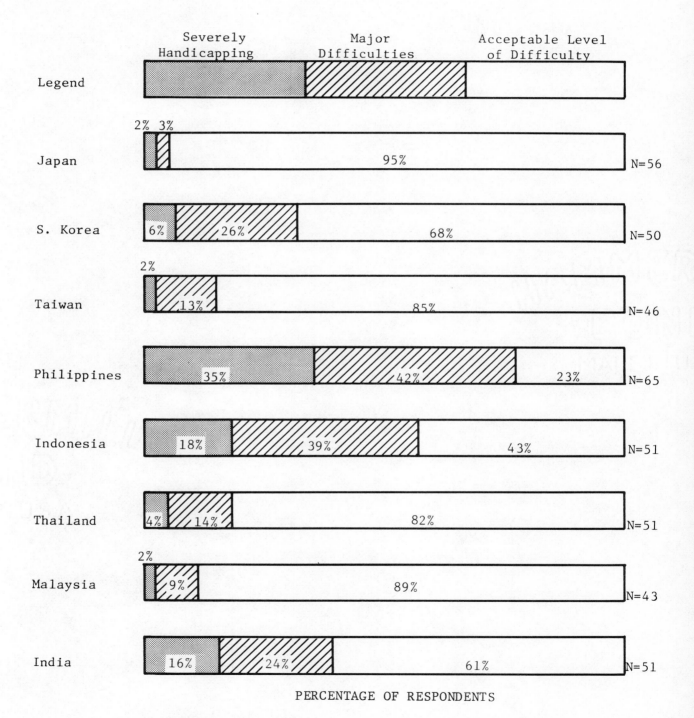

PERCENTAGE OF RESPONDENTS

TOTALS MAY NOT ADD TO 100% BECAUSE OF ROUNDING

GRAPH 30

DISTRIBUTION OF RESPONDENTS' OPINIONS OF THE
EXPECTED LEVEL OF DIFFICULTY TO BE CAUSED BY
ASIAN GOVERNMENTS' CURRENCY INSTABILITY IN 1976

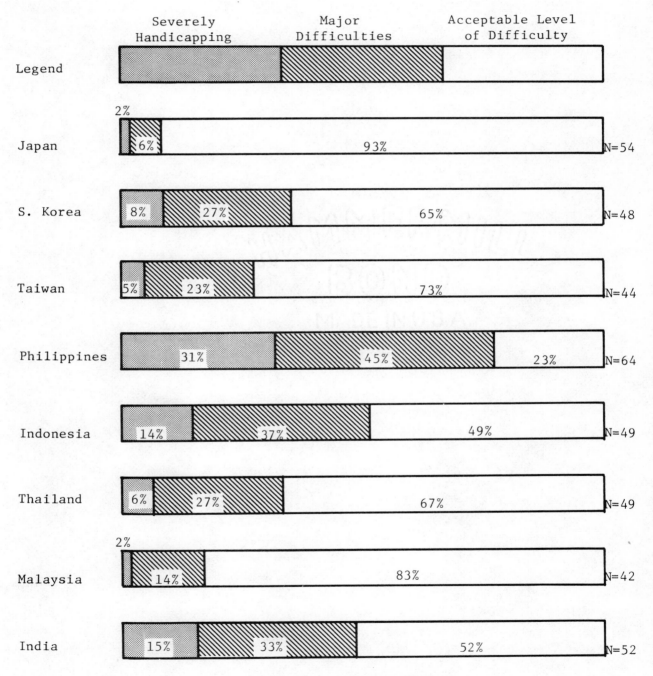

PERCENTAGE OF RESPONDENTS

TOTALS MAY NOT ADD TO 100% BECAUSE OF ROUNDING

present but the situation is expected to worsen in five years. Malaysia presents an acceptable level of difficulty at present and in five years.

In general, currency instability is expected to increase within the next five years in all Asian countries with the exception of Japan.

EARNINGS REMITTANCE POLICY

Host governments often limit the extent of earnings which a foreign company is allowed to remit overseas. This is largely due to balance of payments problems a country may have and a desire to encourage or force foreign companies to engage in additional investments within the host country. However, restrictions on remittance of earnings have a seriously negative effect on a country's investment climate. Graphs 31 and 32 present the views of responding companies on the level of difficulty caused by the earnings remittance policies of Asian countries at present and in five years.

The greatest level of difficulty is being experienced in the Philippines and is expected to continue in the next five years. India follows the Philippines in terms of level of difficulty both at present and in five years. Japan, on the other hand, is viewed as being the least difficult country on this point both at present and in five years. The remaining Asian countries fall somewhere between the Philippines and Japan.

A significant minority of the respondents note major and severe difficulties in South Korea at present and in five years. The response for Taiwan is not appreciably different from the response for South Korea. In Indonesia, respondents are experiencing a relatively higher level of difficulty, which is likely to continue over the next five

GRAPH 31

DISTRIBUTION OF RESPONDENTS' OPINIONS OF
LEVEL OF DIFFICULTY CAUSED BY ASIAN GOVERNMENTS'
RESTRICTIVE EARNINGS REMITTANCE POLICY IN 1971

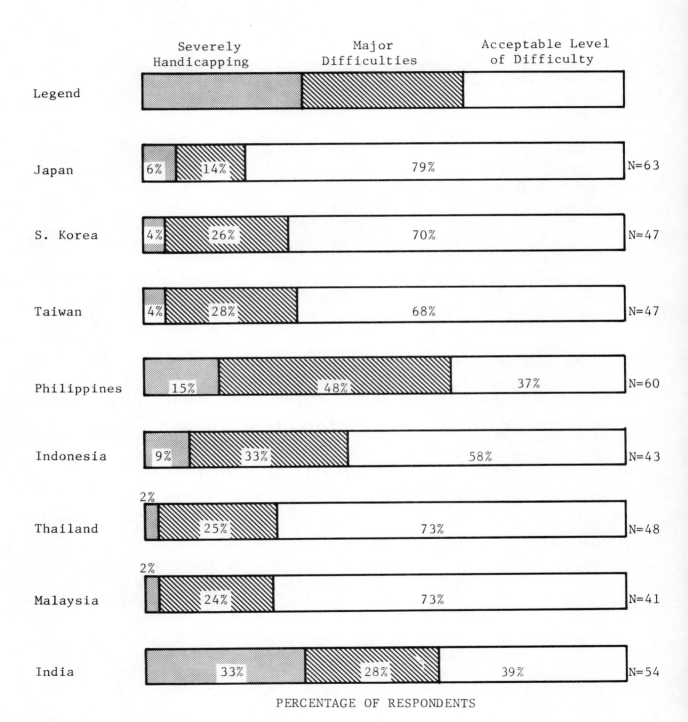

PERCENTAGE OF RESPONDENTS

TOTALS MAY NOT ADD TO 100% BECAUSE OF ROUNDING

GRAPH 32

DISTRIBUTION OF RESPONDENTS' OPINIONS OF
EXPECTED LEVEL OF DIFFICULTY TO BE CAUSED
BY ASIAN GOVERNMENTS' RESTRICTIVE EARNINGS
REMITTANCE POLICY IN 1976

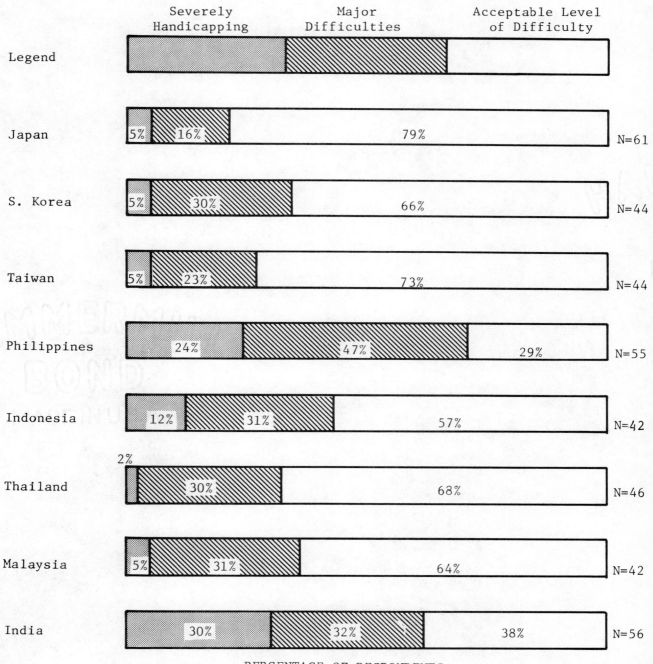

PERCENTAGE OF RESPONDENTS

TOTALS MAY NOT ADD TO 100% BECAUSE OF ROUNDING

years. Thailand and Malaysia are largely at an acceptable level of difficulty and are expected to remain so in five years.

HOST GOVERNMENT PRICE CONTROLS

Host governments often control the prices of essential goods and services. Food items, for instance, frequently fall under this category. Price controls, however, often extend into a wide range of goods and services offered within the local economy. Graphs 33 and 34 show the views of responding executives on the level of difficulty they have experienced at present and expect to encounter in the coming five years in several Asian countries.

The most difficult country on this point is India, both at present and in five years, but the overwhelming majority of the respondents find the level of difficulties in Japan, South Korea, Taiwan, the Philippines, Indonesia, Thailand, and Malaysia acceptable. For all countries, there is a noticeable increase in the major and severely handicapping categories in five years, and responding companies anticipate a growth in price controls instituted by host governments in Asia as a part of their general economic planning and development programs.

IMPORT RESTRICTIONS

In order to conserve foreign exchange and encourage development of indigenous resources, host governments limit the range, extent, and quantity of goods and services a foreign company may import for its operations. The level of such imports changes over time as local resources are developed. At times, however, host governments might insist on the use of local resources, even when they are not compet-

GRAPH 33

DISTRIBUTION OF RESPONDENTS' OPINIONS OF LEVEL OF DIFFICULTY CAUSED BY ASIAN GOVERN- MENTS' PRICE CONTROLS IN 1971

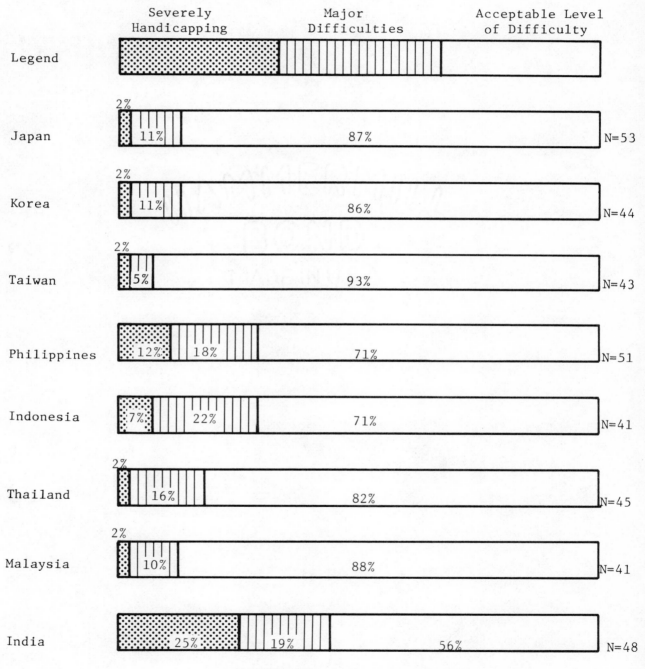

PERCENTAGE OF RESPONDENTS

TOTALS MAY NOT ADD TO 100% BECAUSE OF ROUNDING

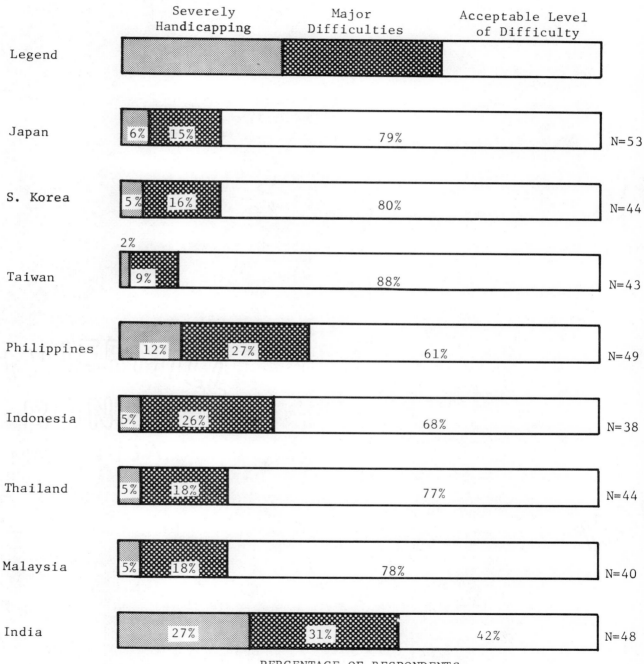

GRAPH 34

DISTRIBUTION OF RESPONDENTS' OPINIONS OF THE
EXPECTED LEVEL OF DIFFICULTY TO BE CAUSED BY
ASIAN GOVERNMENTS' PRICE CONTROLS IN 1976

	Severely Handicapping	Major Difficulties	Acceptable Level of Difficulty
Legend			
Japan	6%	15%	79%	N=53
S. Korea	5%	16%	80%	N=44
Taiwan	2%	9%	88%	N=43
Philippines	12%	27%	61%	N=49
Indonesia	5%	26%	68%	N=38
Thailand	5%	18%	77%	N=44
Malaysia	5%	18%	78%	N=40
India	27%	31%	42%	N=48

PERCENTAGE OF RESPONDENTS

TOTALS MAY NOT ADD TO 100% BECAUSE OF ROUNDING

109

itive in international terms on the basis of price and quality. Of course, these and other considerations pose a severe problem for the foreign company. Graphs 35 and 36 present the views of responding companies on the extent of difficulties they have experienced and anticipate over the next five years in several Asian countries.

Responding companies have experienced the greatest level of difficulty in India with the largest single response falling in the severely handicapping category. No reduction is expected in the next five years. In the view of a majority of respondents, the Philippines is viewed as presenting major and severely handicapping problems at present and in five years. A significant minority of the respondents find major and severely handicapping difficulties in all the other Asian countries. Reference to Graphs 35 and 36, however, suggests that in several countries a majority of the respondents expect a decrease in the level of difficulties in the next five years as a result of import restrictions.

TIME FOR PROJECT APPROVAL

Often it takes considerable time to secure host government approval of a foreign investment in an Asian country. An ambivalent attitude toward foreign investment, local pressure groups, bureaucratic red tape, the nature of the project—these and a host or other reasons often delay the approval of a project. Graph 37 shows the distribution of time it took foreign companies to secure approval of their most recent projects in Asian countries.

The largest response for Japan fell in the 3-7 month category, followed by 7-12 months and 1-2 years. A small percentage secured approval of the Japanese government in less than three months. However, a significant

GRAPH 35

DISTRIBUTION OF RESPONDENTS' OPINIONS OF LEVEL
OF DIFFICULTY CAUSED BY ASIAN GOVERNMENTS'
IMPORT RESTRICTIONS IN 1971

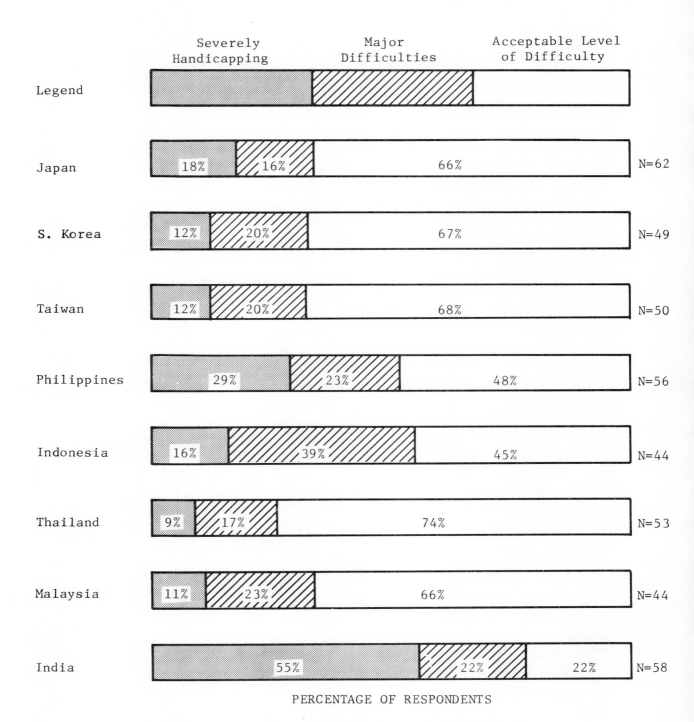

PERCENTAGE OF RESPONDENTS

TOTALS MAY NOT ADD TO 100% BECAUSE OF ROUNDING

GRAPH 36

DISTRIBUTION OF RESPONDENTS' OPINIONS OF THE
EXPECTED LEVEL OF DIFFICULTY TO BE CAUSED BY
ASIAN GOVERNMENTS' IMPORT RESTRICTIONS IN 1976

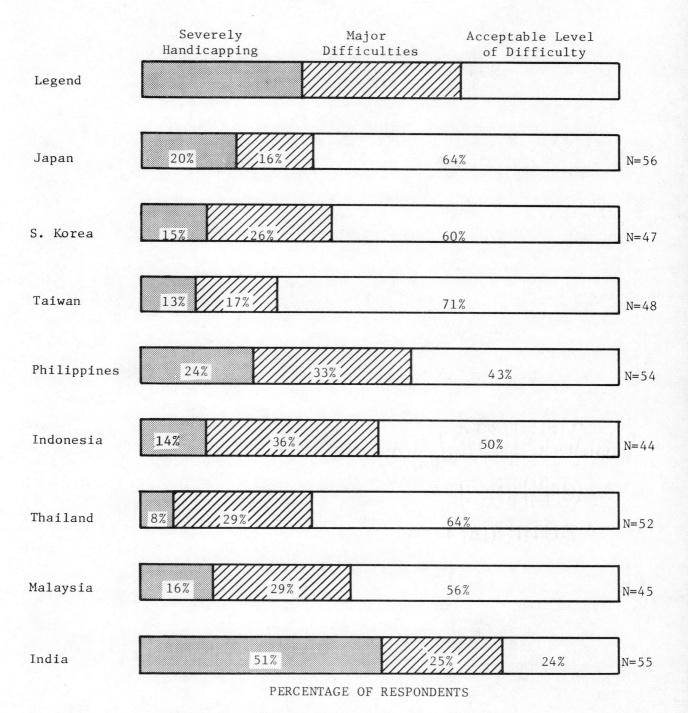

PERCENTAGE OF RESPONDENTS

TOTALS MAY NOT ADD TO 100% BECAUSE OF ROUNDING

minority states that approval can be a question of a year or more.

South Korea reveals a different picture than Japan. Thus, the largest response category is of less than 3 months, followed by 7-12 months and 3-7 months. However, a significant minority spent over a year in securing approval of a project from the host government. In general terms, the picture for Taiwan is not too different from that of South Korea except that almost half of the respondents placed themselves in the less than three months category.

For the Philippines, the largest response fell in the 3-7 months category, followed closely by the less than 3 months category. A significant minority spent 7-12 months and a somewhat lower percentage spent over a year.

For Indonesia, the largest response fell in the 7-12 months category followed by less than 3 months and 3-7 months (with a similar distribution of response). Again, as with some other Asian countries, a sizeable minority spent over a year for approval.

Thailand and Malaysia reveal essentially the same characteristics, the largest response falling in the less than 3 months category, followed by the 3-7 month category.

The picture for India is significantly different. Here, the largest response fell in the over two years category followed by 1-2 years and 7-12 months. A small minority secured approval in less than three months.

A characteristic of most operating problems discussed is that responding companies expect the level of difficulties to increase in the coming five years. Because of this, along with the other restrictions on foreign companies (e.g., extent of ownership, areas of investment),

GRAPH 37

DISTRIBUTION OF RESPONDENTS' OPINIONS OF ASIAN
GOVERNMENTS' APPROVAL TIME CONCERNING INVESTMENT

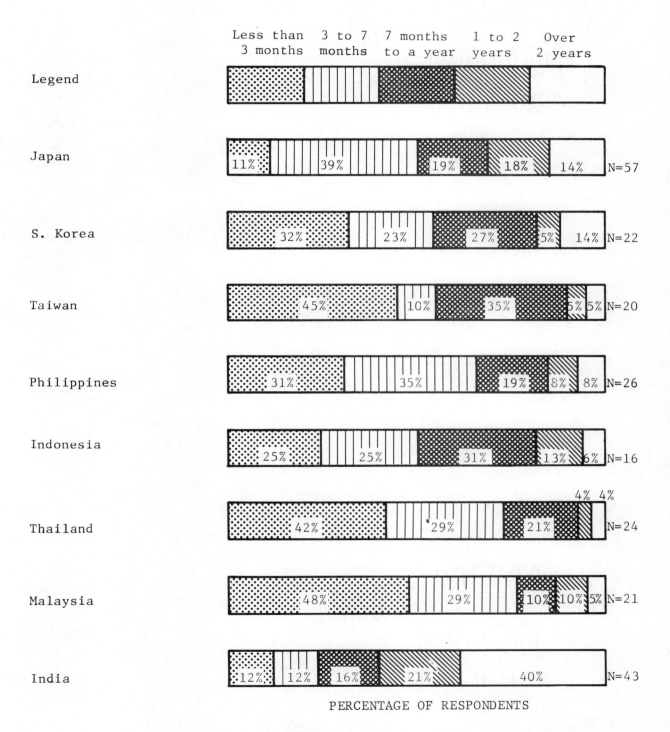

PERCENTAGE OF RESPONDENTS

TOTALS MAY NOT ADD TO 100% BECAUSE OF ROUNDING

managers will need to adopt a more innovative approach to achieve the objectives of the enterprise while still being consistent with the objectives of the host country.

6

The Japanese Challenge in Asia

This chapter shows the extent of Japanese competition experienced by American companies and that expected in five years and the reasons for the competitive strength in Asia of the Japanese.

Of all the Asian countries, Japan has the highest level of industrialization, and a gross national product figure among the largest in the world. During the post-World War II period, the Japanese economy expanded at a fantastic rate. In the 1970s, the Japanese are expected to launch a major offensive in international markets in order to continue their rate of growth. Asia is a logical market for them and has already accounted for a significant percentage of Japanese exports. Also, Asia's raw materials are a strong attraction for a resource-poor country such as Japan. In short, Japanese companies are the major competitors of American companies operating in Asia.

EXTENT OF COMPETITION

Graph 38 shows the extent of competition from Japanese companies at present and anticipated in five years by American companies operating in Asia. Competition is viewed as growing, and is expected to become extremely strong in five years. While a minority consider that the Japanese offer no competition at present, the response in this category diminishes to almost zero in five years. The most dramatic shift is in the category of extremely strong competition. While less than one-third

116

GRAPH 38

DISTRIBUTION OF RESPONDENTS' OPINIONS OF THE
COMPETITION BY JAPANESE COMPANIES AT PRESENT
AND IN FIVE YEARS

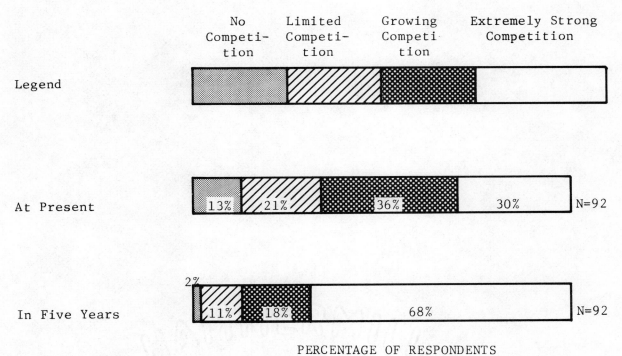

PERCENTAGE OF RESPONDENTS

TOTALS MAY NOT ADD TO 100% BECAUSE OF ROUNDING

GRAPH 39

DISTRIBUTION OF RESPONDENTS' OPINIONS OF JAPANESE COMPANIES' COMPETITIVE ADVANTAGES OVER U.S. COMPANIES IN ASIA IN 1971 AND 1976

N=91 (1971)
N=90 (1976)

REASONS FOR ADVANTAGE

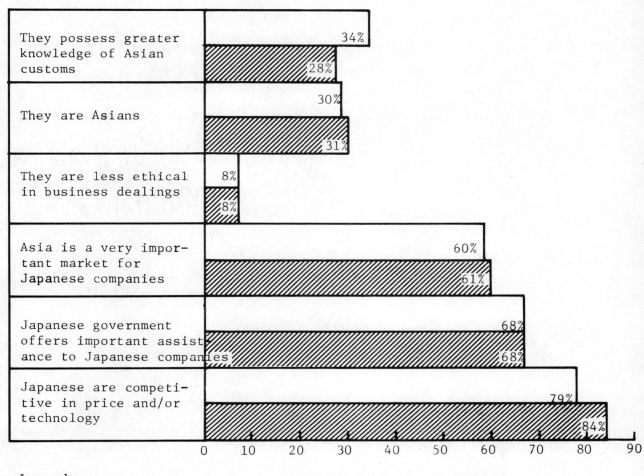

PERCENTAGE OF RESPONDENTS

Legend
1971
1976

TOTALS EXCEED   100% BECAUSE SOME RESPONDENTS
GAVE MORE THAN ONE REASON

of the respondents consider the present level of competition as being extremely strong, over two-thirds expect it to be extremely strong in five years.

REASONS FOR COMPETITIVE STRENGTH

Graph 39 shows the reasons for the competitive strength of the Japanese in Asia. The most important reason is that they are competitive in price and/or in technology of the goods and services they offer to Asian customers; besides, the Japanese offer a range of technologies which is more suited to the particular requirements of Asian countries. The argument is that the Japanese have developed from a war-ravaged nation into a highly industrialized power in less than thirty years and in the process have gone through several different stages of technologies before reaching their present level of advancement. Therefore, they are better equipped to offer less advanced technologies to Asian countries because they are still familiar with them.

The second most important reason is the assistance given by the Japanese government to Japanese companies doing business in Asia. Such assistance takes place in various ways, including Japanese government aid to Asian countries.

The third most important reason is that Asia is a prime market for Japanese companies, and they will want to protect existing markets, as well as develop new ones in Asia.

The fourth reason is that respondents believe that at present the Japanese possess greater knowledge of Asian customs; in five years this advantage will decrease somewhat. The category "greater knowledge of Asian customs" refers to the know-how of the many unique business practices

of each of the Asian countries, and the category "they are Asians" refers to the fact that the Japanese try to promote their business in Asia on the grounds that they are Asians and therefore have a better knowledge and understanding of Asians than Westerners. However, the point is that the Japanese either use their Asian-ness or their actual greater know-how of Asian business to significant advantage.

A very small minority of respondents stated that the competitive strength of the Japanese in Asia is due in part to the fact that they are less ethical in business than Americans.

The overall implication is that the Japanese will offer intense competition, and their competitive strength is based on a series of reasons which are not likely to decline in importance in the coming years.

7

Plans for the Future

This chapter presents the plans that responding companies expect to put into effect in the next five years by American companies operating in Asia: namely, the extent to which companies plan to change (increase, decrease) their present level of investments in Asia; the specific Asian countries in which they plan to undertake new and/or additional investments; and the type of investment they plan to make on a country-wide basis.

PROPOSED ADDITIONAL INVESTMENT

Graph 40 shows that, while a small minority of companies (13%) plan to maintain the present level of investment, the overwhelming majority (86%) plan to increase their investments in Asia over the next five years. Only one company plans to reduce its existing level of investment.

The distribution of the response for the companies planning to increase investments reveals some interesting features. Thus, 15% plan to increase investments in the next five years by over 75% of their present level. Nearly 34% of the responses fell in the 11-25% category; 20% in the 26-50% category; 18% in the 0-10% category; and 3% in the 51-75% category.

The growth plans of American companies permit some observations:

GRAPH 40

DISTRIBUTION OF RESPONDENTS' OPINIONS OF
CHANGE OF INVESTMENTS IN ASIA

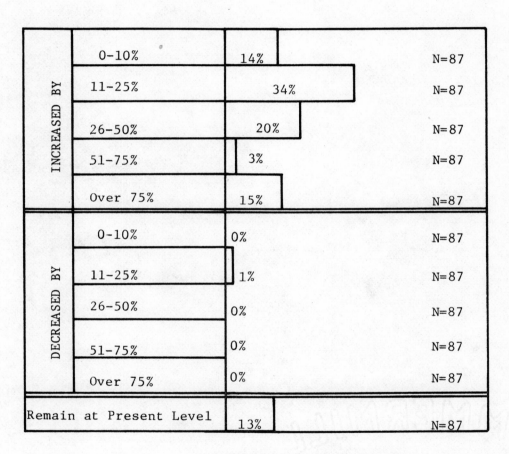

PERCENTAGE OF RESPONDENTS

1)   The overwhelming majority of companies planning an increase in investments clearly indicates that <u>a large number of companies are interested in Asia</u> as a place of operations. For those responding companies which already have operations in Asia, the increase in investments would result in a higher level of commitment (from sales office to licensing to manufacturing) and a greater geographic scope, i.e., establishing operations in a larger number of Asian countries.

2)   The plans for increased investment reveal that <u>American companies consider the overall investment climate</u> at present and in five years <u>to be favorable.</u>

3)   <u>Increased investment</u> planned by American companies <u>might take place toward the earlier, rather than later, phase of the five-year period.</u> The increasing restrictions expected by American companies in the case of some Asian countries may encourage them to make the investment before the restrictions actually take effect. Conversely, in the case of certain other Asian countries in which companies do not expect a significant change in the overall investment climate, companies are likely to feel comfortable in making new or additional investments in the near future. American companies may also wish to invest before competitors get there because Japanese companies are already highly interested in Asian markets.

DISTRIBUTION OF NEW AND/OR ADDITIONAL INVESTMENT

In which Asian countries are American companies likely to make additional and/or new investments? Graph 41 shows the distribution of response, and reveals at the same time a company's evaluation of the investment climate of a given country. In general, the more favorable the investment climate,

GRAPH 41

DISTRIBUTION OF RESPONDENTS' OPINIONS OF
NEW AND/OR ADDITIONAL INVESTMENTS
EXPECTED WITHIN THE NEXT FIVE YEARS

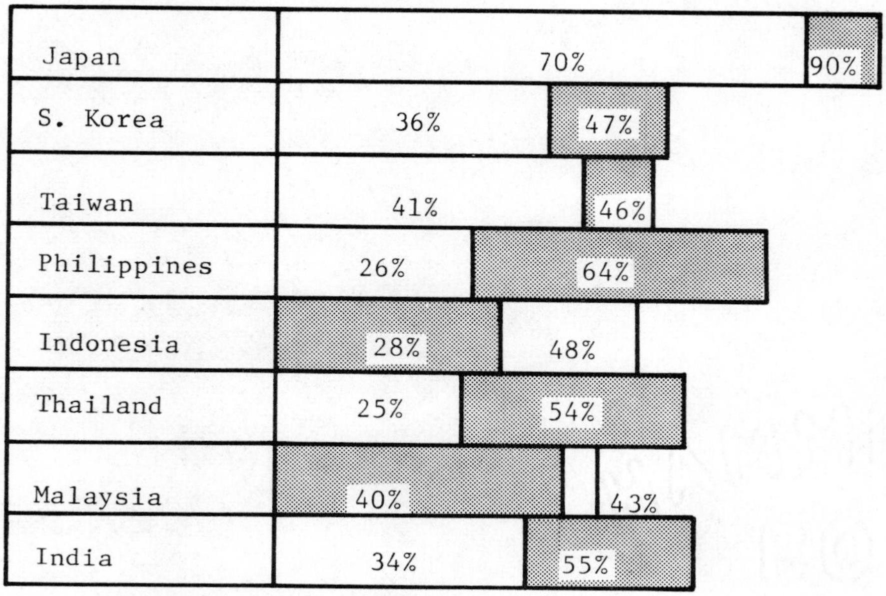

Japan	70%	90%
S. Korea	36%	47%
Taiwan	41%	46%
Philippines	26%	64%
Indonesia	28%	48%
Thailand	25%	54%
Malaysia	40%	43%
India	34%	55%

N=80 (unshaded area)
N=89 (shaded area), taken from Graph 4.

124

the greater the likelihood of that country attracting foreign private investments.

The information in Graph 41 should be interpreted in conjunction with other considerations relevant to investing abroad. If, for example. a company wishes to achieve a better regional balance in its operations, it might invest in countries which rank lower than others in terms of investing.

Graph 41 shows that Japan will remain the primary objective of new/ additional investments by American companies in the coming five years. South Korea, which ranks fifth in the existing distribution is not expected to change in five years. Taiwan, however, which is in sixth place at present is expected to move up to the third rank. [This survey was made before the People's Republic of China was admitted into the United Nations and before the United States changed its policy toward the PRC.] The Philippines shows a dramatic decline, from second at present to seventh. Indonesia, on the other hand, is expected to move from seventh to second place. Thailand shows a significant decline, from fourth position to eighth place in five years. Malaysia, on the other hand, shows the opposite picture, moving from the lowest rank of eight at present to the rank of four. India shows a decline from third to sixth place in five years.

TYPES OF INVESTMENTS IN THE FUTURE

Graph 5 shows the distribution of the responding companies by types of investments. Graph 42 shows the types of new/additional investments expected within the next five years.

Comparison of the two graphs (5 and 42) reveals some interesting

GRAPH 42

DISTRIBUTION OF RESPONDENTS' OPINIONS OF TYPES OF
INVESTMENTS EXPECTED WITHIN THE NEXT FIVE YEARS

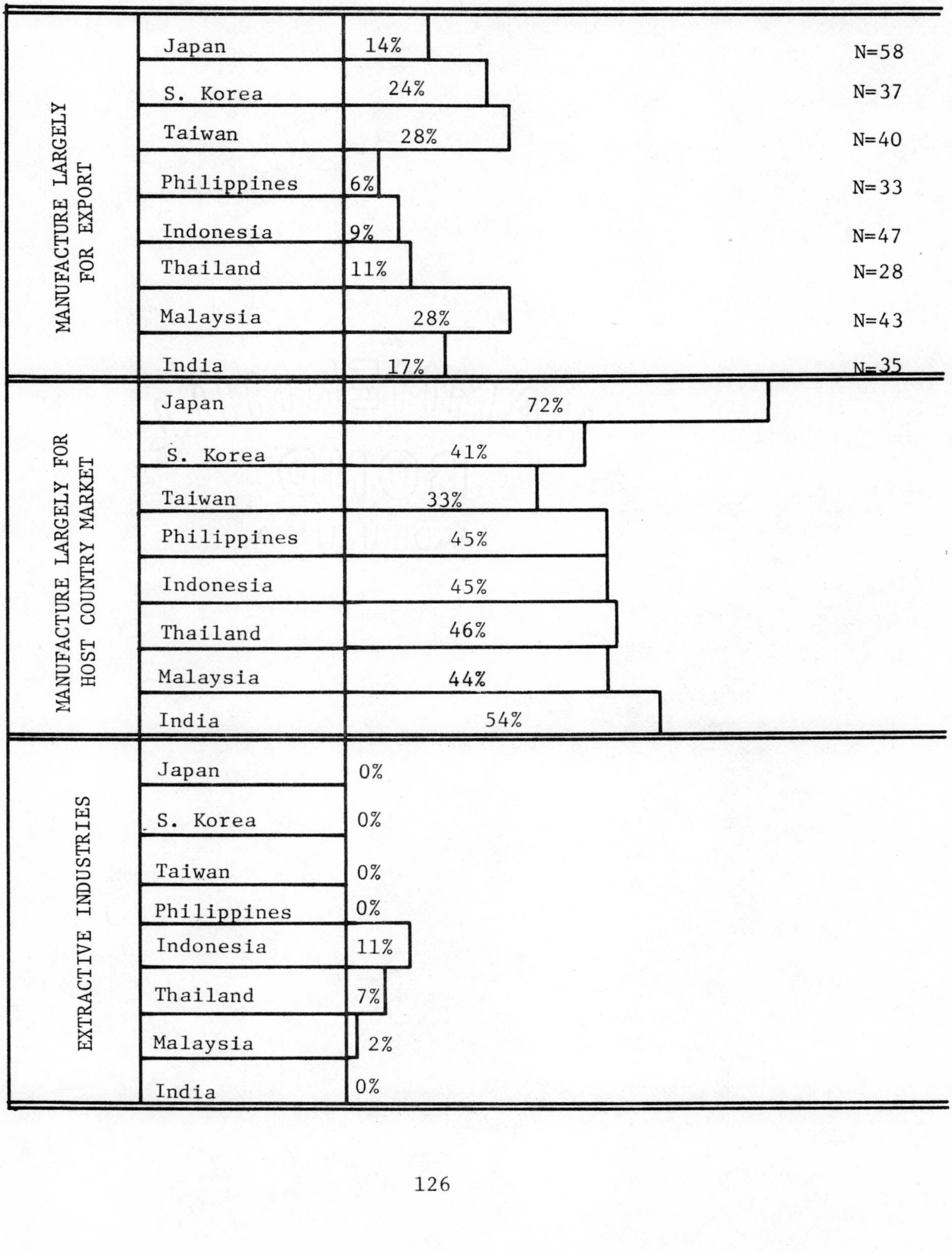

MANUFACTURE LARGELY FOR EXPORT

Country	%	N
Japan	14%	N=58
S. Korea	24%	N=37
Taiwan	28%	N=40
Philippines	6%	N=33
Indonesia	9%	N=47
Thailand	11%	N=28
Malaysia	28%	N=43
India	17%	N=35

MANUFACTURE LARGELY FOR HOST COUNTRY MARKET

Country	%
Japan	72%
S. Korea	41%
Taiwan	33%
Philippines	45%
Indonesia	45%
Thailand	46%
Malaysia	44%
India	54%

EXTRACTIVE INDUSTRIES

Country	%
Japan	0%
S. Korea	0%
Taiwan	0%
Philippines	0%
Indonesia	11%
Thailand	7%
Malaysia	2%
India	0%

GRAPH 42 (continued)

MANAGEMENT SERVICES CONTRACTS		
Japan	5%	
S. Korea	14%	
Taiwan	8%	
Philippines	6%	
Indonesia	17%	
Thailand	18%	
Malaysia	14%	
India	14%	

DISTRIBUTORSHIP		
Japan	16%	
S. Korea	16%	
Taiwan	23%	
Philippines	21%	
Indonesia	19%	
Thailand	21%	
Malaysia	21%	
India	6%	

LICENSE AGREEMENT		
Japan	24%	
S. Korea	24%	
Taiwan	28%	
Philippines	27%	
Indonesia	21%	
Thailand	21%	
Malaysia	19%	
India	37%	

127

GRAPH 42(continued)

OTHER		
Japan	5%
S. Korea	5%
Taiwan	8%
Philippines	15%
Indonesia	13%
Thailand	7%
Malaysia	5%
India	3%

PERCENTAGE OF RESPONDENTS

TOTAL FOR A COUNTRY MAY EXCEED 100% BECAUSE SOME RESPONDENTS GAVE MORE THAN ONE REASON

features. Thus, in nearly all countries, the new/additional investments will be increasingly export-oriented. The primary reason for the new/ additional investment, however, will continue to be that of catering to the host-country market. Management services contracts are expected to gain in importance, especially in the countries of Southeast Asia. License agreements are expected to decrease in Japan, but they show a significant increase in all other Asian countries.

8

OBSERVATIONS

The Asian region is evolving in many dimensions, and a far greater
body of research than we have now is required for a complete des-
cription of the Asian investment climate. Nevertheless, the results
of this questionnaire, coupled with field research both in Asia and
in the United States, may serve as a guide for corporate executives
and host-government officials in the formulation of policies and
programs.

GREATER RESTRICTIONS ON FOREIGN INVESTMENTS

One of the major trends revealed by the questionnaire is that, with
the possible exception of Japan, all the Asian countries included in
this study will impose greater restrictions on foreign direct investment,
and greater pressure will be exerted by host governments on foreign
investors, in future, to use indigenous resources and to place emphasis
on exports.

The pace at which host governments will impose restrictions on
foreign investments is greater than indicated by the responding com-
panies--a point which is clearly indicated in discussions with many
government officials, local businessmen, intelligentsia, students, and
political leaders in Asia. A significant implication of this gap in
the relative pace of change expected by the foreign investor and the

changes sought by host governments is that it will increase the level of conflict between the two parties.

The growing mood toward restrictiveness by host countries has several implications for the foreign investor:

First, he will have to understand and contend with a continuous reduction of incentives or concessions offered to the foreign investor at the time of entry. The terms applicable to new investments will be reassessed with the objective of reducing the extent of foreign participation in the coming years. In essence, the foreign investor must always bear in mind that the terms of investment will be subject to sudden change. Therefore, success depends on the ability to anticipate and adapt to changing situations with a minimum of conflict.

Second, limitations on the extent of foreign ownership will result in a gradual reduction of management control by the foreign company. This will become a problem especially for the multinational enterprise which seeks coordination and integration of its worldwide operations. Inability to retain effective management control over the Asian operations will not permit as effective an integration as sought by the multinational enterprise.

Third, a critical requirement for the investor will be the need to employ executives who understand and can cope with the existing and emerging Asian problems. There are not many presently working for American companies. And more restrictive policies and the desire of American companies to expand in Asia will require a thorough understanding of specific Asian countries on the part of executives.

Fourth, for host governments the main question will not be whether the foreign investor can make a contribution to their development objec-

tives. The investor clearly does make a contribution. The critical question, however, will be for Asian governments to evaluate realistically the nature and extent of contributions from the foreign enterprise in the light of their development objectives. Unrealistic demands or dependence on the foreign investor will not be helpful.

Fifth, a critical determinant of the relationship between Asian governments and international enterprises will be how well both parties make a systematic and concerted effort to develop and utilize various channels of communication with each other. In the future, the need for a considered dialogue between the two parties will become more important as the potential for conflict between them increases. Failure by either party to keep channels of communication open will contribute to greater conflict.

POLICIES BEFORE THE FACT

In Latin America strongly adverse reaction toward foreign investments has occurred <u>after the fact</u> of fairly large amounts of investments by American companies. However, direct investment by American companies in Asia is still quite limited. Greater restrictions on foreign investments on the part of Asian governments is occurring <u>before the fact</u> of significant growth in U.S. investment.

A major implication of this feature in Asia is that it affords both the international enterprise and the host governments breathing space for a careful review and consideration of their respective programs of action. However, the lull is likely to last only a few years because, unlike Latin America, most Asian countries have a long history of colonialism, and conflicts over economic issues may trigger a nationalistic reaction against foreign investors.

American companies have encountered significant problems in Latin America. In planning for their Asian operations, they should reflect upon the experience and accordingly formulate policies which might tend to avoid similar conflicts in the Asian context.

INTERNATIONAL MIXED VENTURES

In many countries, Asian governments will be playing a growing role not only as regulators but also as investment partners. At present, American companies do not favor such partnerships. However, given a definite trend in this direction, the foreign investor, especially in capital-intensive and strategic industries, will have to recognize the inevitability of such combinations, and may well benefit from them. If a company takes the lead in developing innovative approaches, it will have a greater chance of securing more favorable terms than when submitting to enforced change. Japanese and European companies are far more receptive to collaborations with governments, and American companies will have greater pressures placed on them to move in this direction.

Host governments will have to be more specific about their intentions with regard to their objective to monitor a project, to control it, or to train nationals in the public sector. Different countries will have different objectives, depending on the nature of the industry. As with private sector entrepreneurs, government officials who serve as executives in mixed or public-sector enterprises will also seek an extension of their range of activities, resulting in a growth of mixed-venture activity.

A partnership with a host government is only one form of participation. Other arrangements are likely to occur wherein a foreign

company uses a variety of forms in the same country. For example, it might have a collaboration with the host government in a particular product, associate itself with private interests in other areas, and offer purely technical assistance in yet additional areas. Some of the projects might be on a minority basis, others on a majority basis, and still others with no equity interests at all. The point is that various types of investments--joint ventures, licensing, management contracts, turnkey arrangements, etc.--will continue to operate in Asia. Foreign companies will need to combine one or more of these methods in keeping with the emerging requirements of countries within the region.

ERA OF NEGOTIATIONS

Both corporate executives and host government officials realize that the only way to understand the nature of the conflict and solve it is through negotiation. Both parties also recognize that conflicts are not limited to any particular industry or issue or region. They are inclined to learn from each experience.

The international enterprise will have to place greater emphasis on working toward compromise solutions. Furthermore, success will depend on the availability of executives who are skilled in the art of negotiating within the Asian context.

In future, the frequency of negotiations between the foreign investor and host governments will increase, and the issues will become more sub-jective and elusive (dealing with questions of contributions by the enter-prise to the host society). Such issues will be more difficult to resolve because they will be more difficult to define.

INDIGENOUS BUSINESSMEN AS AN INTEREST GROUP

In all Asian countries, indigenous businessmen are a major pressure group seeking an ever-growing range of privileges and business activities. Accordingly, there will be increasing pressure from indigenous businessmen to reduce the foreigner's activities in favor of indigenous groups. Indigenous groups will also seek participation even in areas of endeavor in which the foreigner is clearly the logical source of resources. Given the importance of the indigenous business community, the foreign company will have to seek its support.

THE JAPANESE PRESENCE

Japanese political and economic strength will grow in the coming years. Although there is a body of adverse reaction toward the Japanese in Asian countries for historical reasons, the Japanese will be treated by the emerging generation of decision makers on the same basis as are other foreign investors by the host governments. In this respect, it will be the policies and approaches of the Japanese enterprise which will determine the nature of the reaction they generate in Asia.

The Japanese have traditionally been isolated from the rest of the world. Nevertheless, the coming decade promises to be one in which Japanese foreign direct investments will become a major force especially in Asia. The big question will be whether the Japanese can adapt and modify their business approaches and objectives to fit the requirements of host societies.

*   *   *   *

135

The foregoing discussion should not be interpreted as a pessimistic assessment of the Asian region from a foreign investment standpoint. Both the foreign investor and the host governments will profit if they adopt a realistic attitude of what each can offer to the other. Unfortunately, in Asia as in other parts of the world, the frequent tendency of host-government officials and of foreign executives alike is to ignore the realities of the situation. In the process, false expectations are aroused, and soon relations between both parties begin to deteriorate. Both the foreign investor and the host government must be realistic about each other's needs and capabilities; only when such an understanding is achieved can serious and continuous relations become a reality.

The foregoing discussion should not be interpreted as a pessimistic assessment of the Asian region from a foreign investment standpoint. Both the foreign investor and the host governments will profit if they adopt a realistic attitude of what each can offer to the other. Unfortunately, in Asia as in other parts of the world, the frequent tendency of host-government officials and of foreign executives alike is to ignore the realities of the situation. In the process, false expectations are aroused, and soon relations between both parties begin to deteriorate. Both the foreign investor and the host government must be realistic about each other's needs and capabilities; only when such an understanding is achieved can serious and continuous relations become a reality.

9

American Business and the China Market*

During the past year, American businessmen have expressed a keen
interest in the prospects for trade with the 800 million citizens
of the People's Republic of China (also known as Mainland China,
China, or the PRC). The major impetus for such an interest was the
move toward political rapproachment by the U.S. government dramatized
by President Nixon's visit to China in February, 1972.

China is a major political force in Asia, and Asian countries
are acutely conscious of the shifting relationship between the U.S.
and the PRC--a relationship which has implications for their own
approach vis-à-vis the PRC. The problems and prospects both from the
standpoint of international relations and international business are
largely unknown at present. The only realistic, and safe, statement
to offer at this stage is that the PRC will play an increasingly
important political and economic role in Asia and in international
relations in general. During the past two decades, U.S. companies
have had no commercial interests in the PRC; the situation has now
changed dramatically. In the future, American companies will need to
recognize the commercial prospects of the PRC in planning for their
Asian and for their worldwide operations.

*This chapter has been developed by Ashok Kapoor with the assistance of
 Richard Schmitt.

TRADE WITH THE PEOPLES'S REPUBLIC OF CHINA: AN OVERVIEW

For more than twenty years, the U.S. government barred American companies and their foreign subsidiaries from all trading activities with the PRC. Considerable pressure was also brought to bear by the U.S. government on other non-Communist nations to participate in the embargo with the objective of inhibiting China's economic and political growth and thus, possibly, contribute to the downfall of its Communist government. The embargo was, in its totality, considerably more severe in its restrictions on trade with the PRC than the laws restricting trade with the Soviet Union and other European Communist nations. But the embargo proved to be largely ineffective, since China was able to obtain the desired imports initially from the Soviet Union and other Communist nations and more recently from several free world nations who elected to discontinue participation in the U.S.-sponsored embargo.

As more and more non-Communist nations began trading with China, and the level of this trade increased ($1.4 billion with non-Communist nations in 1968), the U.S. government was pressured by American companies and other groups interested in promoting better relations with the PRC to reconsider its policies.

In July 1969 President Nixon announced the first of a series of moves intended to greatly reduce U.S. government restrictions on trade with China:

July 1969	American tourists allowed to purchase $100 of Chinese goods for personal use.
	Restrictions on travel to China relaxed.
December 1969	$100 ceiling removed on tourist purchases.
	Foreign-based affiliates of U.S. firms permitted to purchase raw materials from

Mainland China as long as these are not
for export to the U.S.

April 1970

U.S.-made components and related spare parts
selectively licensed for use in foreign
goods exported to China.

August 1970

U.S. oil companies abroad permitted to
service free-world ships bearing non-
strategic cargoes to Chinese ports. Fuels
sold could not be of U.S. origin.

March 1971

All travel restrictions lifted on Americans wishing to visit China.

April 1971

Visas granted to Chinese applying to visit
the U.S.

U.S. currency controls relaxed to permit
use of U.S. dollars by China.

Restrictions ended on American oil companies
providing U.S. fuel to ships or aircraft
proceeding to and from China, except on
Chinese-owned or chartered vessels bound to
or from North Vietnam, North Korea, or Cuba.

U. S. vessels or aircraft allowed to carry
Chinese cargoes between non-Chinese ports;
U.S.-owned, foreign-registered vessels per-
mitted calls at Chinese ports.

President Nixon requests inter-agency committee representing U.S. departments of State,
Commerce, Agriculture, and Treasury to prepare
a list of non-strategic items to be placed
under general license for direct export to
China.

Direct imports of designated Chinese items
authorized.

May 1971

List of goods which may be freely exported
to China released. Forty-seven categories
of goods included covering most non-strategic
items produced in the U.S., such as most
farm products, fish, lumber, fertilizer,
coal, metals, chemicals, automobiles, agricultural equipment, household appliances
and light industrial, and roadbuilding
equipment. These may be sold to China
without any special, official license.

139

February 1972	President Nixon visits the People's Republic of China.
April 1972	U.S. businessmen invited to participate in the Canton trade fair.
July 1972	White House approved Boeing Company's application for sale of several Boeing 707 jets to the PRC.

Despite the relaxation, the existing restrictions on U.S. trade with the PRC are greater than those governing trade with the Soviet Union or Eastern European countries. Items such as locomotives, petroleum products, navigation equipment, and machinery for welding large pipes are some of the items excluded from the free list even though these products may be sold to the Russians. However, the government is pursuing a flexible policy as evidenced by White House approval of the sale of Boeing 707 jets to the PRC.

As a result of a greater rapprochement, more and more products from the PRC are finding their way into the U.S. market. For the most part these are consumer products such as cameras, ping-pong balls and paddles, porcelainware, and art objects and vases. Total two-way trade is on the order of $4 million.

The direction and conduct of foreign trade by the PRC has both political and economic overtones. The overall objectives of her foreign trade policy are:

1) To strengthen the economic independence and sovereignty of the state, protecting domestic industry and agriculture from the economic aggression of imperialist powers.

2) To serve the development of China's industry, particularly heavy industry.

3) To achieve economic self-reliance.

4) To serve as a weapon for international political struggle.

A fundamental aspect of the PRC's economic policies is to become self-reliant, and to prevent any form of foreign domination. China's history is replete with exploitations of her resources by foreign powers, which makes the current leadership extremely wary of any such recurrence.

The fourth policy objective, mentioned before, is exemplified by the four conditions set forth by Premier Chou En-Lai for Japanese firms desiring to trade with the PRC, namely:

1) They must not invest in Taiwan or South Korea.

2) They must not trade with Taiwan or South Korea.

3) They must play no role in the Indochina War.

4) They must not be affiliated with U.S. firms as partners or sub-sidiaries.

The PRC has applied these conditions on a flexible basis depending upon its ability to get comparable goods and prices from other countries. China trades with many non-Communist nations which have not extended official diplomatic recognition to the PRC. In other cases she provides generous foreign aid to those areas of the world where she hopes to extend her influence. Under certain conditions the political aspects of foreign policy are made subservient to the economic goals.

As in the case of the Soviet Union and Eastern European countries, the PRC handles foreign trade strictly through government organizations which contract for the purchase and sale of goods according to their overall development plans. The American company wishing to do business with China will not have direct contact with the end users of its products and services (unlike business in the rest of the world). Instead, it will be dealing only with government officials. (A listing of the various trade organizations and the products handled by them is available from the U.S. Department of Commerce.)

What is the extent of China's trade with non-Communist countries, and what are the estimates of the volume of trade with the United States? Table 8 presents the volume of exports from 11 non-Communist countries to the PRC in 1969 and in 1970.

TABLE 8

EXPORTS TO MAINLAND CHINA FROM ELEVEN COUNTRIES*
(U.S. $ in millions)

	1969	1970
Total Exports to China of the Countries listed	$1,162	$1,264**
Japan	391	625
West Germany	158	152
Australia	157	NA
United Kingdom	135	111
Canada	113	145
France	74	72
Italy	67	65
Netherlands	23	24
Belgium	16	25
Switzerland	16	22
Sweden	12	23

*Third National Convocation on the Challenge of Building Peace, courtesy of Mr. Jack Perry, Chairman, London Export Corp. Ltd.

**Excludes Australia

Professor Robert F. Derenberger concludes after an extensive study of the potential of trade between the U.S. and the PRC that China's current partners should be able to supply her import demands and absorb

her export commodities, except for textiles. Thus, China will be under no internal economic pressure to trade with the U.S. Consequently, the level of trade with the U.S. will depend upon the ability of U.S. firms to compete with China's current trading partners in regard to product quality, price, and terms of sale.

Professor Derenberger provides the following range of estimates for 1980 of the potential value of trade between the U.S. and the PRC:

Pessimistic	$25 million each way
Neutral	$200 million each way
Optimistic	$325 million U.S. exports
	$200 million U.S. imports

This assumes that in 1980 China would still limit its level of imports to its export potential, estimated at $4.9 billion. At this level of imports, Professor Derenberger projects that minerals and metals will comprise 30% of the total, machinery and equipment 25%, and chemicals 15%.*

In brief, observers of the PRC economy have expressed reservations about the volume of two-way trade which can be generated during the 1970s. Even a highly optimistic estimate of $325 million in exports by 1980 is a minuscule sum compared to the overall exports from the United States. Yet, American companies remain interested and attracted by the potential of PRC markets.

---

*Arvind V. Phatak, ed. *Building Business Bridges to Eastern Europe and Mainland China* (Philadelphia: School of Business Administration, Temple University, 1972).

The objective of the study is to determine the subjective expectations
of American executives regarding the trade potential with the People's
Republic of China. More specifically, the following questions are
explored:

1) Market Penetration Objectives: What are the objectives of
American companies in attempting to penetrate the markets of the PRC?

2) Interest and Market Potential: What is the extent of interest
of American companies at present and in five years in the markets of the
PRC, and what are the primary reasons for this interest? What is the
market potential for the goods and services of American companies in the
PRC?

3) Level of Trade: What are the factors influencing the level of
trade between the U.S. and the PRC?

4) Sources and Type of Information: What are the sources of information used by American companies in investigating the markets of the PRC?
What type of information is sought by American companies?

5) Market Penetration Methods: What methods of market penetration
(export, licensing, turnkey projects, etc.) are American companies
planning to use? What sources (U.S., Asian, elsewhere in the world) are
American companies likely to use to penetrate the markets of the PRC?

6) Competition: What are the primary sources of competition for
American companies attempting to do business with the PRC?

It should be stressed that the primary emphasis is on the subjective
expectations of American executives. This is particularly relevant in the
case of the PRC because most American companies have either not formulated,

or are only in the initial stages of formulating, their policies and approaches toward the PRC markets. And as is true of most decisions in international business, the subjective expectations of executives will play a critical role in a company's approach to PRC markets.

METHODOLOGY

This chapter is based on the results of a questionnaire survey of 442 U.S. companies. A total of 95 companies responded--a response rate of 21%. The questionnaires were mailed to executives in the U.S. shortly after President Nixon's return from the PRC in order to permit the responding executives to think through the implications of the visit for U.S.-PRC trade. Out of the 442 companies in the mailing, 386 companies were from Fortune's list of top 500 U.S. industrial companies with verifiable international operations, and 56 other companies known to have interests in Asia.

POSITION OF RESPONDENTS

Of the responding executives, 85% identified themselves according to position. The breakdown is as follows:

Chairman of the Board	1
President	10
Executive Vice President	2
Vice President	21
Director	7
Controller	1
Manager	11
Supervisor	1
"Assistant to"	8
Secretary	1

Most respondents were from the senior levels of management who would play an important role in their company's policies and program of action toward the PRC.

SALES VOLUME

The distribution of responding companies by annual sales volume in 1971 is:

Sales	No. of Respondents
Less than $200 million	16
$200-300 million	10
$301-600 million	21
$601-1,000 million	14
$1,001-2,000 million	15
Over $2,000 million	16
Other--Banks	3
Total	95

TRADE PRODUCTS

Responding companies listed two or three products they would particularly want to export to the PRC. The product groups are presented below by SITC:

Group	No.* of Respondents
Food and Live Animals	4
Beverages and Tobacco	0
Crude Materials, Inedible, Except Fuels	3
Mineral Fuels, Lubricants, and related materials	7
Animal and Vegetable Oils and Fats	0
Chemicals	21
Manufactured Goods Classified By Material	10
Machinery and Transport Equipment	26
Miscellaneous Manufactured Articles	21
Commodities and Transactions not Classified According to Kind	12
Total	104

---

*The number of products exceeds the number of responses as at times the two or three listed products belonged to different categories.

146

The categories with the highest number of responses were machinery and transport equipment, miscellaneous manufactured articles, and chemicals, and these reflect the major categories that Professor Derenberger projected would constitute China's imports in 1980.

*THE RESPONSE**

<u>Objectives of American Companies</u>. For most American companies the markets of the PRC are largely unknown in terms of size, needs, and the process of how to sell to the Chinese. Nevertheless, a company must have certain objectives in its desire to sell its products and services to a foreign country--for example, to be part of a larger worldwide network, to cater to host-country markets, or to earn royalties and dividends. In the case of China, the range of objectives which an American company can logically pursue are limited by the terms and conditions under which foreign companies are permitted to do business with the PRC. Thus, direct investments for ownership of local operations are entirely excluded. But what are the objectives of American companies in attempting to do business with the PRC--to export, to sell technology, to buy, or a combination of objectives?

Graph 43 presents the distribution of objectives of responding companies at present and in five years. At present, the most important objective is to <u>export</u> to the PRC, with particular emphasis on exports of machinery, equipment and finished goods, followed by exports of U.S. raw materials and semi-finished goods. Following closely behind these categories

---

*The response to the questions were cross-tabulated according to size (in terms of annual sales) and product category to determine if there were any significant differences in response, but the analysis did not reveal any meaningful changes in response and is therefore not incorporated in this study.

is the sale of technology. The other categories of response (export to the PRC from third countries, i.e., from Asian affiliate; obtain raw materials; and export to third-country markets) follow at some distance.

In five years, the responding companies in general do not expect their objectives to change significantly. The export of machinery, equipment and finished goods remains the most important objective. Only the sale of technology moves into second place, in five years, followed by export of raw materials and semi-finished goods.

This response suggests that American companies propose to emphasize the development of bilateral trade with the PRC--i.e.,engage in direct export of U.S. products and know-how and direct import of Chinese products and services--and is supported by the far lower importance attached to catering to PRC markets from "third countries" such as Japan, Canada, or Hong Kong.

An important reason for this approach might be that corporate executives believe they can exercise greater control under bilateral trade than when third parties are brought into the picture, as is often the case when unknown and potentially important markets are to be opened up. In addition, very few executives, including those in Asia, have significant know-how vis-à-vis the PRC. This feature encourages corporate management to play the leading role, at least during the initial stages of market development.

Purchasing raw materials from the PRC is a far less important objective. Because of the Chinese practice of balanced two-way trade with a foreign trading partner, American companies might not be able to sell as much to the PRC unless they can buy an almost equivalent quantity from the PRC. Raw material purchases do not seem to be the

GRAPH 43

KEY OBJECTIVES OF U.S. COMPANIES

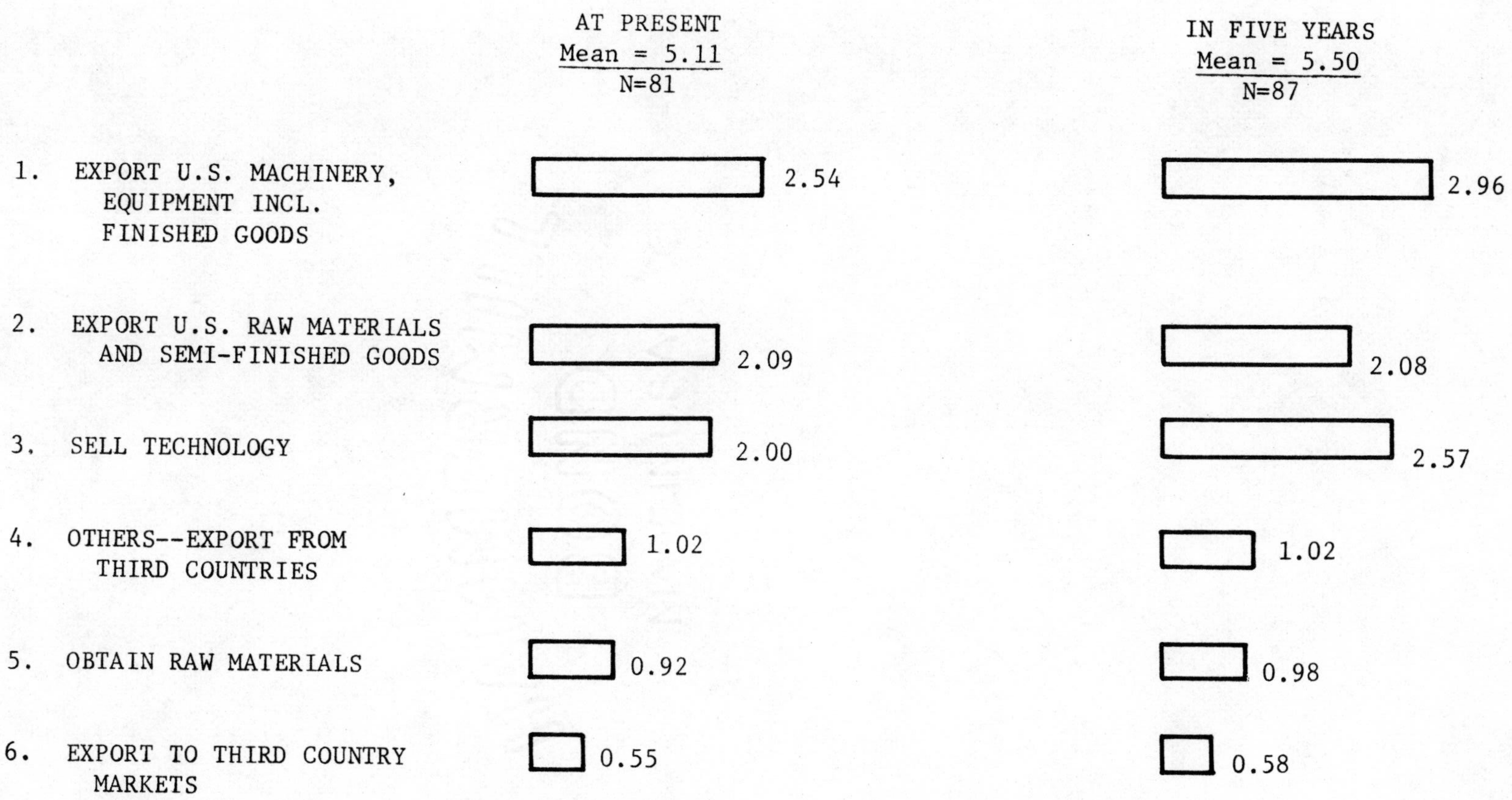

AT PRESENT
Mean = 5.11
N=81

IN FIVE YEARS
Mean = 5.50
N=87

1. EXPORT U.S. MACHINERY, EQUIPMENT INCL. FINISHED GOODS
2.54
2.96

2. EXPORT U.S. RAW MATERIALS AND SEMI-FINISHED GOODS
2.09
2.08

3. SELL TECHNOLOGY
2.00
2.57

4. OTHERS--EXPORT FROM THIRD COUNTRIES
1.02
1.02

5. OBTAIN RAW MATERIALS
0.92
0.98

6. EXPORT TO THIRD COUNTRY MARKETS
0.55
0.58

answer. Finished and semi-finished goods might contribute toward reducing the trade gap.

INTEREST IN PRC MARKETS

Level of Interest. The political rapprochement with the PRC came as a surprise for many people, including businessmen. Now the business community has been infected with a mood of expectation of what the rapprochement can mean in terms of trade with the PRC. That the initial expectations were perhaps too exaggerated has been revealed by the ensuing set of events and in particular by the fact that to date only a handful of relatively insignificant concrete transactions have been concluded with the PRC.

The purpose here is to determine whether American companies have a strong and continuing interest in PRC markets. If they do, it entails a different approach than if the interest is largely or exclusively on the order of a "passing fancy." Needless to say, even at present there is a "bandwagon effect" which obliges companies to imitate their competitors so as to avoid the impression of being left out of what might prove to be a profitable market. The coming years will tend to weed out many companies in this category.

The response of companies on their level of interest at present and in five years in the PRC markets is presented in Graph 44. At present, the largest response (51%) is for the limited interest category, followed by 27% for strong interest and 12% for very strong interest. Only 10% of the responding companies stated that they had no interest in PRC markets at present.

The picture changes rather dramatically in five years: not a single

responding company stated that it was not interested in the markets of the PRC. And the largest frequency of response (57%) occurs for the category of strong interest, followed by 27% stating a very strong interest, and only 16% falling under the limited interest category. In brief, American companies reveal a significant growth of interest in the next five years in the markets of the PRC.

Graph 44 suggests that companies have a strong and sustained interest which is endorsed by the fact that many of the companies falling under the strong and very strong categories at present are the same ones falling under these categories in five years. Additionally, a significant percentage of companies in the limited and no interest categories at present advance to the higher levels of interest in five years. Thus, the responding companies are viewing the PRC markets from a long term standpoint and not as a "flash in the pan."

Reasons for level of interest. What are the primary reasons for the level of interest at present and in five years? The choice of responses falls into two broad categories--either generally favorable or unfavorable to a high level of interest. Thus, relaxation of U.S. government restrictions, the presence of considerable demand in the PRC at present, and potentially large markets in the future are conducive to greater interest. Keeping up with the actual or potential moves of competitors forces companies to develop interest in the PRC market. The negative considerations, however, include the many unknowns of doing business in the PRC, the small size of the actual and potential markets, and the existence of more profitable opportunities in other countries where a company can utilize its resources.

GRAPH 44

LEVEL OF INTEREST OF RESPONDING COMPANIES IN
PRC MARKETS AT PRESENT AND IN FIVE YEARS

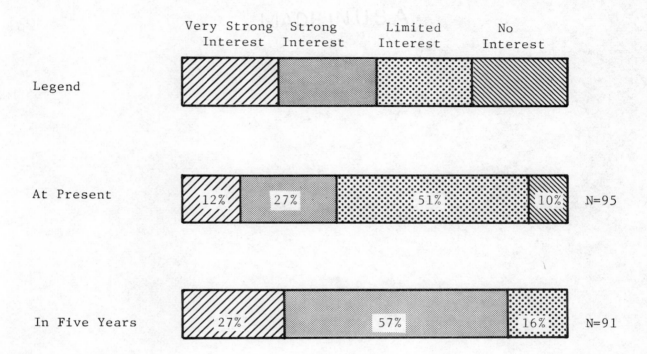

Graph 45 presents the response. The most important reason why companies are interested in PRC markets at present is the relaxation of U.S. government restrictions on trade with the PRC, followed by the presence of a potentially large market. However, considerable demand at present is relatively far less important a reason for interest in PRC markets.

The most important reason deterring American companies are the many unknowns of doing business with the PRC, followed by the presence of more profitable opportunities in other countries and the small size of the actual and potential markets in the PRC. At present, companies assign relatively far less importance to keeping up with the moves of competitors.

In five years, the "Reasons for Level of Interest" differ significantly from those expressed for the present. By far the most important reason is the potentially large market in the PRC, while relaxation of U. S. government restrictions becomes a poor second. This point is further endorsed by the response on the small size of the actual and potential market which declines significantly in importance in five years.

Inherent in the strong expectation of a potentially large market in the PRC is the belief that political relations between the U.S. and the PRC will continue to encourage trade between the two countries.

Also, in five years companies expect their competitors to be more actively interested in the PRC. This characteristic is another important reason for the growth of interest in PRC markets.

The reasons discouraging interest in PRC markets decline significantly in importance in five years, and the many unknowns of doing business with the PRC drops sharply in importance. This is understandable since American companies will have greater knowledge of the PRC through their own

GRAPH 45

MAIN REASONS FOR LEVEL OF INTEREST

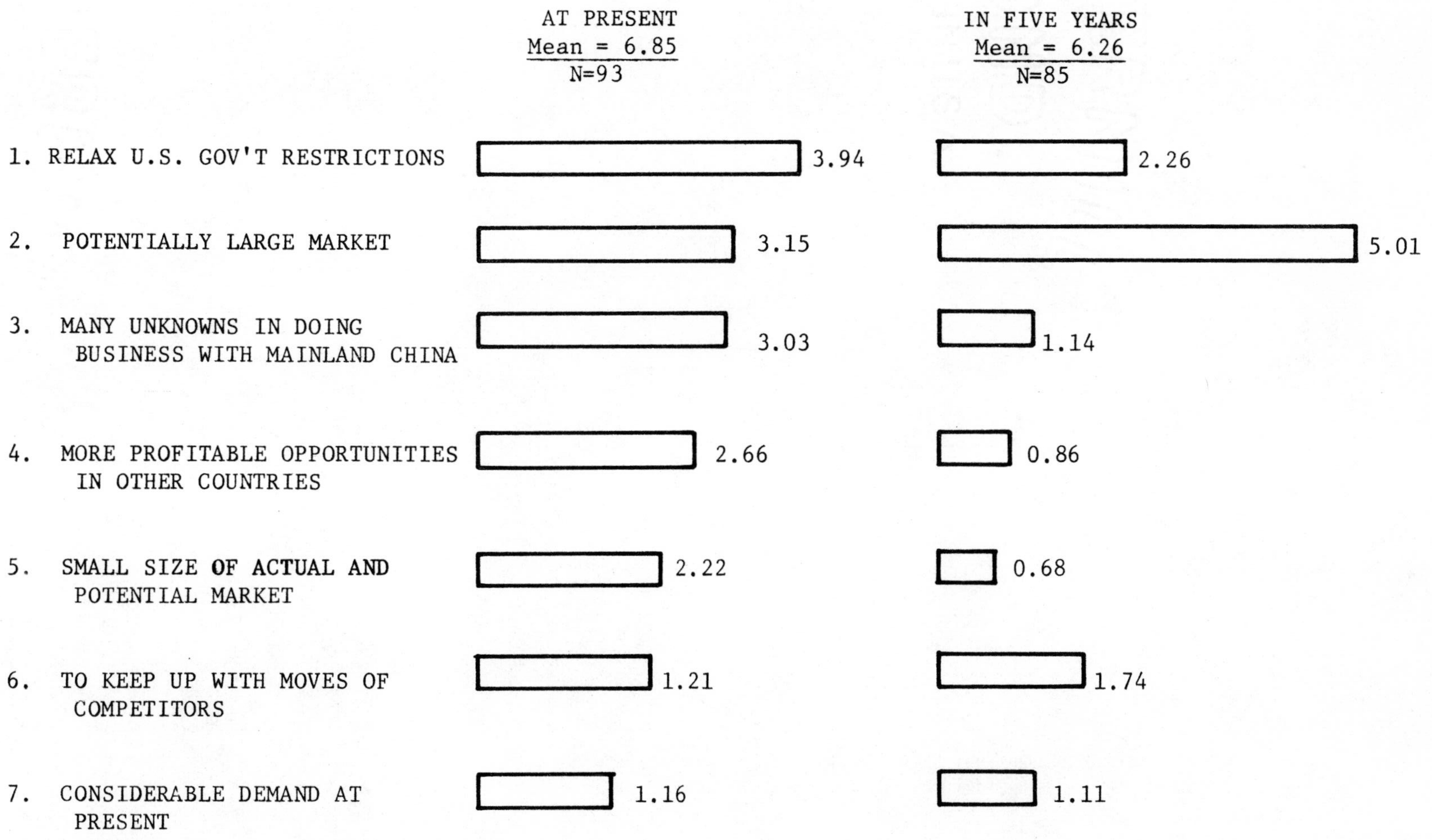

AT PRESENT
Mean = 6.85
N=93

IN FIVE YEARS
Mean = 6.26
N=85

1. RELAX U.S. GOV'T RESTRICTIONS — 3.94 / 2.26

2. POTENTIALLY LARGE MARKET — 3.15 / 5.01

3. MANY UNKNOWNS IN DOING BUSINESS WITH MAINLAND CHINA — 3.03 / 1.14

4. MORE PROFITABLE OPPORTUNITIES IN OTHER COUNTRIES — 2.66 / 0.86

5. SMALL SIZE OF ACTUAL AND POTENTIAL MARKET — 2.22 / 0.68

6. TO KEEP UP WITH MOVES OF COMPETITORS — 1.21 / 1.74

7. CONSIDERABLE DEMAND AT PRESENT — 1.16 / 1.11

experiences, through experiences of competitors, and through larger and more up-to-date information provided by the U.S. government, foreign governments, and the government of the PRC, especially since it became a member of the United Nations.

More profitable opportunities in other countries will become a far less important reason for not considering the PRC markets in five years. This will not mean that profitable opportunities will suddenly cease in other countries. It suggests that companies will attach particular importance to the opportunities available in the PRC for their particular products and services.

In brief, the essential point highlighted by Graph 45 is that American companies expect a significant growth of interest in PRC markets because of a potentially large market for their goods and services requiring a strong and sustained interest over a period of time.

MARKET POTENTIAL

As discussed above, American companies are attracted to the PRC particularly for its potentially large markets based on a huge population of 800 million people, growing emphasis on development, and the acknowledged need for imported goods and services. What is the potential for the goods and services American companies would like to sell to the PRC? (Of course, this can be different from the goods and services that the PRC wishes to import from foreign sources in keeping with its overall development plans.)

The response below is stated in terms of high, medium, low, and no demand. This approach is used because concrete figures on overall imports of particular goods and services, or local manufacture in PRC, do not exist or generally are not available to most American companies. American

companies do not have historical sales information on which to base their estimates of market potential.

Graph 46 offers the response of companies. At present, the highest response (60%) falls under the low-demand category with medium and high demand collectively accounting for 25%. Another 15% fall under the category of no demand. In five years, the highest response is for the category of medium demand (54%) followed by 28% in high demand and 17% in low demand. Only 1% of the companies fall under the category of no demand.

In general, there is a relationship between the level of interest and estimates of market potential. Graphs 44 and 46 show that the frequency distribution for level of interest is generally similar to the distribution for market potential, though interest tends on the whole to be stronger than would be justified by the market potential. The same characteristics appear to apply in five years.

FACTORS INFLUENCING U.S.-PRC TRADE

American companies have a strong and sustained interest in PRC markets which is due largely to expectations of significant market potential for their products and services. However, trade between the U.S. and the PRC will be influenced by a variety of considerations. For the volume of trade to grow as expected, factors favorable to U.S.-PRC trade must predominate over those inhibiting it. The choice of responses was broadly divided into two categories—factors controlled by the PRC (emphasis on faster economic growth; moderate, international leadership; and the ability of China to export to the U.S.) and those largely controlled by the U.S. (further relaxation of U.S. restrictions on trade with

GRAPH 46

ESTIMATES OF MARKET POTENTIAL IN THE PRC:
AT PRESENT AND IN FIVE YEARS

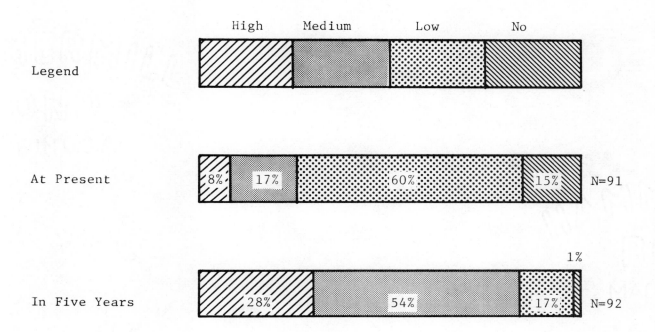

157

the PRC, availability of credit, and withdrawal of support for Taiwan).
Lastly, the factor under the control of American companies was aggressive
selling.

Graph 47 presents the distribution of response on the relative
importance of these factors in determining the level of trade with the
PRC at present and in five years. At present, companies believe that
economic growth and the continuity of a moderate, internationally-
oriented leadership in the PRC will be the most important determinants
of the extent of U.S.-PRC trade. However, further relaxation of U.S.
restrictions will also contribute to trade. The other reasons (ability
of China to export to the U.S., availability of medium- and long-term
credit, withdrawal of U.S. support for Taiwan, and aggressive selling
efforts by U.S. companies) are presented in declining order of importance.

In five years, companies indicate some changes in the relative
importance of factors influencing U.S.-PRC trade. The first two reasons
(emphasizing economic growth and moderate, internationally-oriented
leadership) will remain as important. However, relaxation of U.S. government restrictions will decrease in importance, which might be partly
based on the expectations of companies that most of the restrictions on
PRC trade will be dropped in the next five years. The ability of the
PRC to export, however, gains in importance revealing a concern on the
part of companies that they might not be able to buy goods and services
from the PRC with a market in the U.S. Growing emphasis is placed on
availability of medium- and long-term credit and on aggressive selling
by companies. It should be noted that withdrawal of U.S. support for
Taiwan, while not an important consideration at present, is expected
to decline greatly in importance in five years. (Some observers strongly

GRAPH 47

FACTORS INFLUENCING EXTENT OF TRADE WITH THE PRC

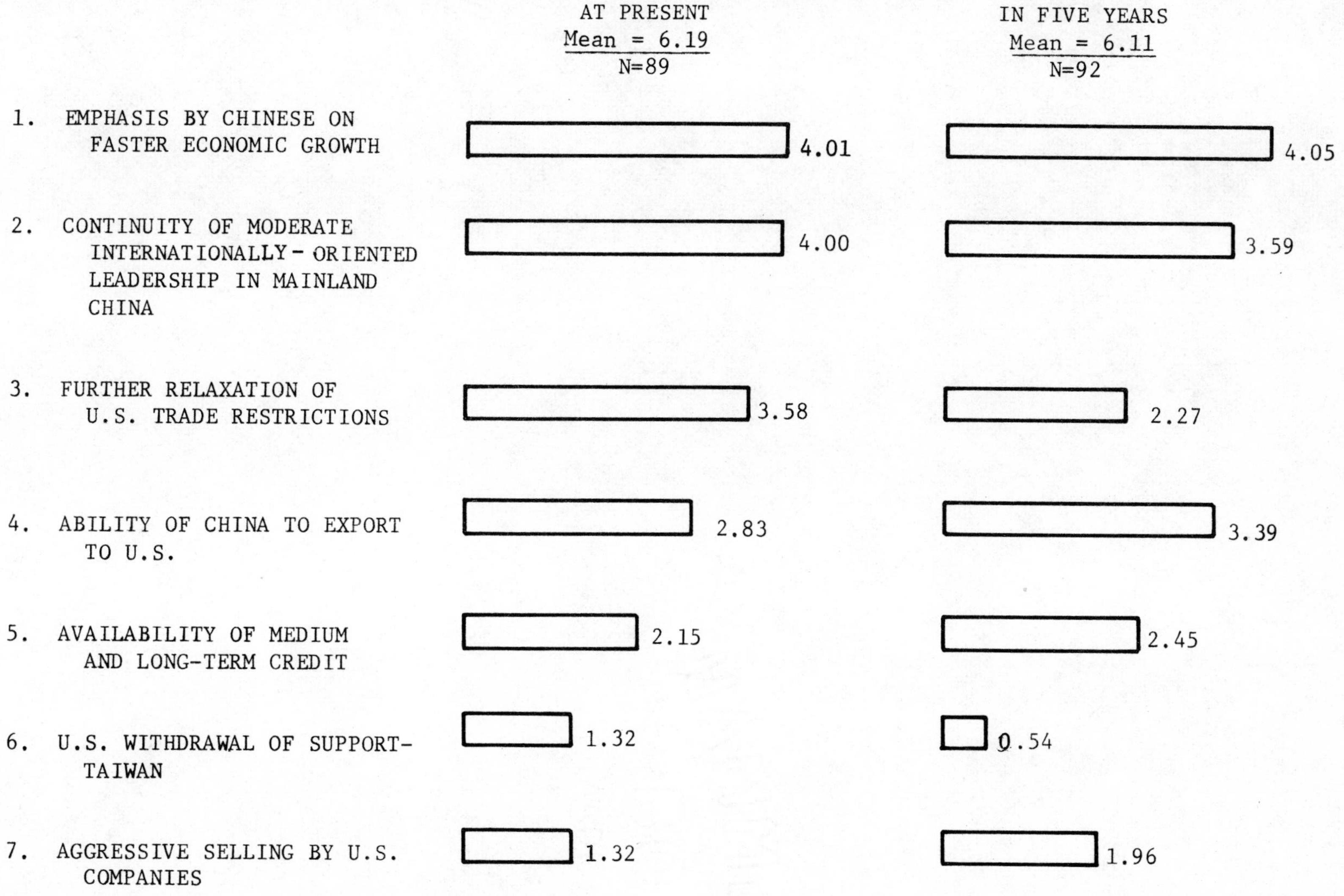

AT PRESENT
Mean = 6.19
N=89

IN FIVE YEARS
Mean = 6.11
N=92

1. EMPHASIS BY CHINESE ON FASTER ECONOMIC GROWTH — 4.01 / 4.05

2. CONTINUITY OF MODERATE INTERNATIONALLY-ORIENTED LEADERSHIP IN MAINLAND CHINA — 4.00 / 3.59

3. FURTHER RELAXATION OF U.S. TRADE RESTRICTIONS — 3.58 / 2.27

4. ABILITY OF CHINA TO EXPORT TO U.S. — 2.83 / 3.39

5. AVAILABILITY OF MEDIUM AND LONG-TERM CREDIT — 2.15 / 2.45

6. U.S. WITHDRAWAL OF SUPPORT-TAIWAN — 1.32 / 0.54

7. AGGRESSIVE SELLING BY U.S. COMPANIES — 1.32 / 1.96

159

hold to the view that the PRC will not engage in any meaningful level of trade with the U.S. until the Taiwan question is resolved.)

The major determinant of U.S.-PRC trade both at present and in five years is expected to be the policies and preferences of the host country, namely, the PRC. In comparison, policies of the U.S. government are expected to play a relatively minor role.

INFORMATION ON DOING BUSINESS WITH THE PRC

An important limitation of U.S. companies is that they do not have access to the type, quantity, or quality of information on the PRC that they are accustomed to before engaging in such international business activities. Relatively little is known about the PRC by American companies, and this situation further increases the importance of accurate and timely information. Additionally, at the initial stages of exploring a market, companies tend to be particularly careful in soliciting information from various sources because the actions they take within the first year or so will largely stamp their subsequent efforts.

Sources of information. How do companies rank the various sources of information (which they use) about the PRC? Typically, companies use more than one source in order to corroborate and verify the information they receive. Their response is presented in Graph 48.

The most important sources of information are their own executives in Asia. They are close to the scene and have access to organizations and individuals with significant experience in trading with the PRC, particularly in Hong Kong. Executives in Asia, therefore, are being asked by top management to keep an eye on PRC markets. Several companies have

160

set up their own "China watchers" in Hong Kong. Having access to information is a major source of power. This characteristic suggests that companies might place particular emphasis on using their Asian operations as a means of exploring PRC markets.

The U.S. government through the departments of Commerce and State is the second most important source of information, but mainly for executives in the U.S. The Department of Commerce has been particularly active in releasing a series of publications designed to assist the businessman in understanding the characteristics of the PRC markets.

Experienced trading companies are ranked as the third most important source of information on the PRC. Often such companies are English, and have a long history of trading with the PRC. American companies therefore recognize their limited know-how and that sound professional advice and guidance will be necessary in exploring PRC markets especially during the initial stages, until such time that the company develops its own body of expertise. The relatively frequent use of in-house studies indicates a move in building internal expertise. This preference also explains the relatively lower importance attached to individual consultants as sources of information. Unfortunately, the dramatic outburst of interest in the PRC on the part of American companies encouraged the appearance of several individuals and organizations claiming to have an expertise on PRC markets—when this was far from being the case. American companies appear to be far more reluctant to proceed with such individuals and organizations, and they rely, rather, on more established, experienced, and dependable organizations.

GRAPH 48

RANKING ON SOURCES OF INFORMATION ON THE PRC

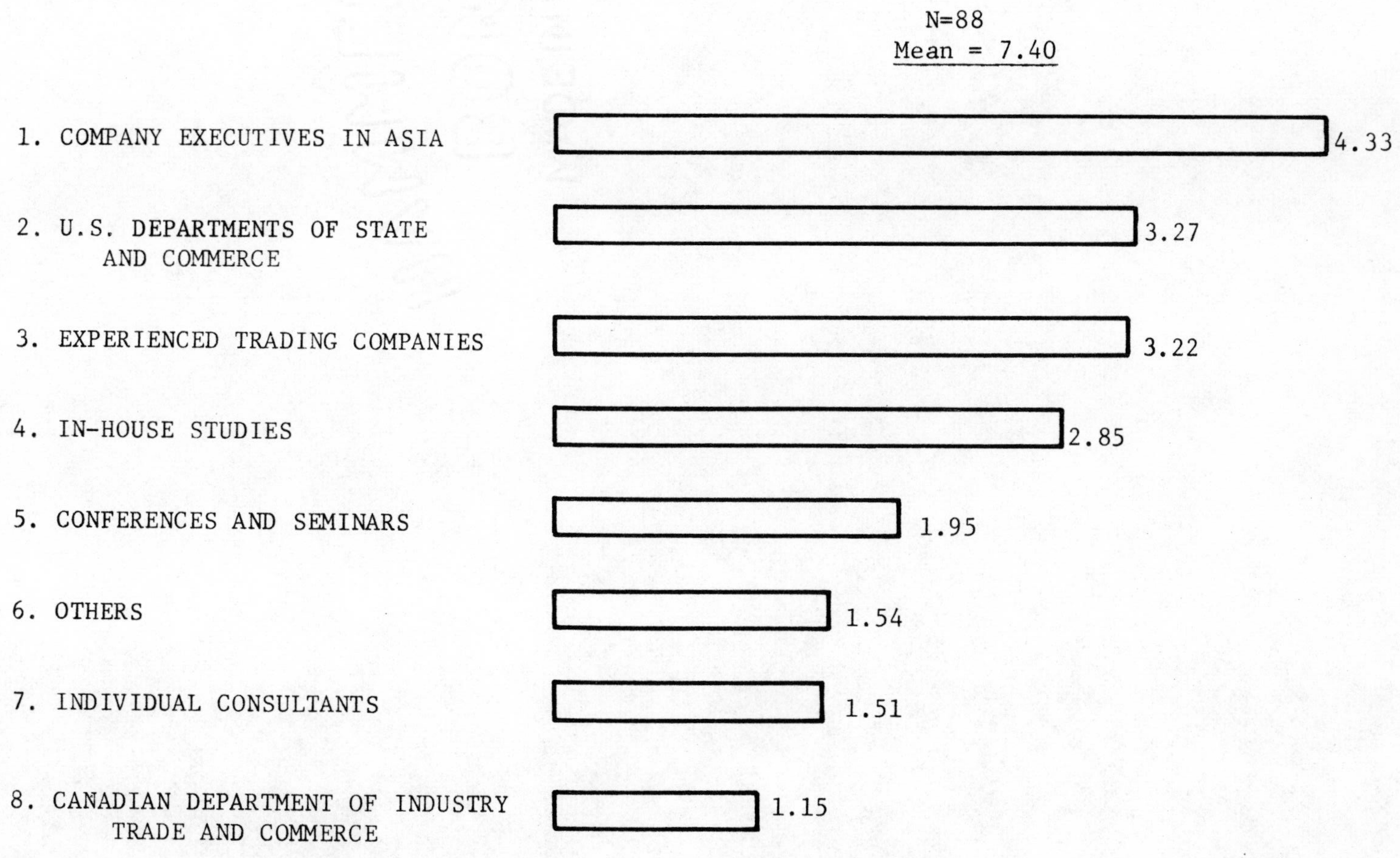

N=88
Mean = 7.40

1. COMPANY EXECUTIVES IN ASIA — 4.33

2. U.S. DEPARTMENTS OF STATE AND COMMERCE — 3.27

3. EXPERIENCED TRADING COMPANIES — 3.22

4. IN-HOUSE STUDIES — 2.85

5. CONFERENCES AND SEMINARS — 1.95

6. OTHERS — 1.54

7. INDIVIDUAL CONSULTANTS — 1.51

8. CANADIAN DEPARTMENT OF INDUSTRY TRADE AND COMMERCE — 1.15

162

Companies are faced with many unknowns in doing business with the PRC. Their need for information about the PRC is therefore greater than for information with which they are more familiar. But what types of information are sought by companies? Graph 49 presents the response.

Companies assign by far the greatest importance to information about estimates of demand for specific products and services. Effective planning for market penetration requires such information. Yet this is most difficult to secure not only for the PRC but for most countries, particularly the developing ones.

The second most important type of information required is how to negotiate with officials of the PRC organizations concerned with foreign trade. Chinese officials, not the end users, negotiate with foreign companies. Host-government officials of course possess a great deal of bargaining strength since their decisions will determine whether a company can enter into the PRC markets. This pattern is similar to ones in the Soviet Union and Eastern European countries.

How to initiate contacts with PRC officials ranks third in importance. The lack of diplomatic relations between the U.S. and the PRC adds to the difficulties of locating the right officials to contact. It is also difficult to determine which trading organization is appropriate for a particular product or service or which individual within the organization should be contacted. Yet companies must have such information to interact effectively with PRC officials.

Terms and conditions of financing rank fourth in importance. As specific transactions are made in the future, financing will become important, as has proven to be the case in trade with the Soviet Union

GRAPH 49

TYPES OF INFORMATION ON THE
PRC SOUGHT BY COMPANIES

Mean = 5.44
N=86

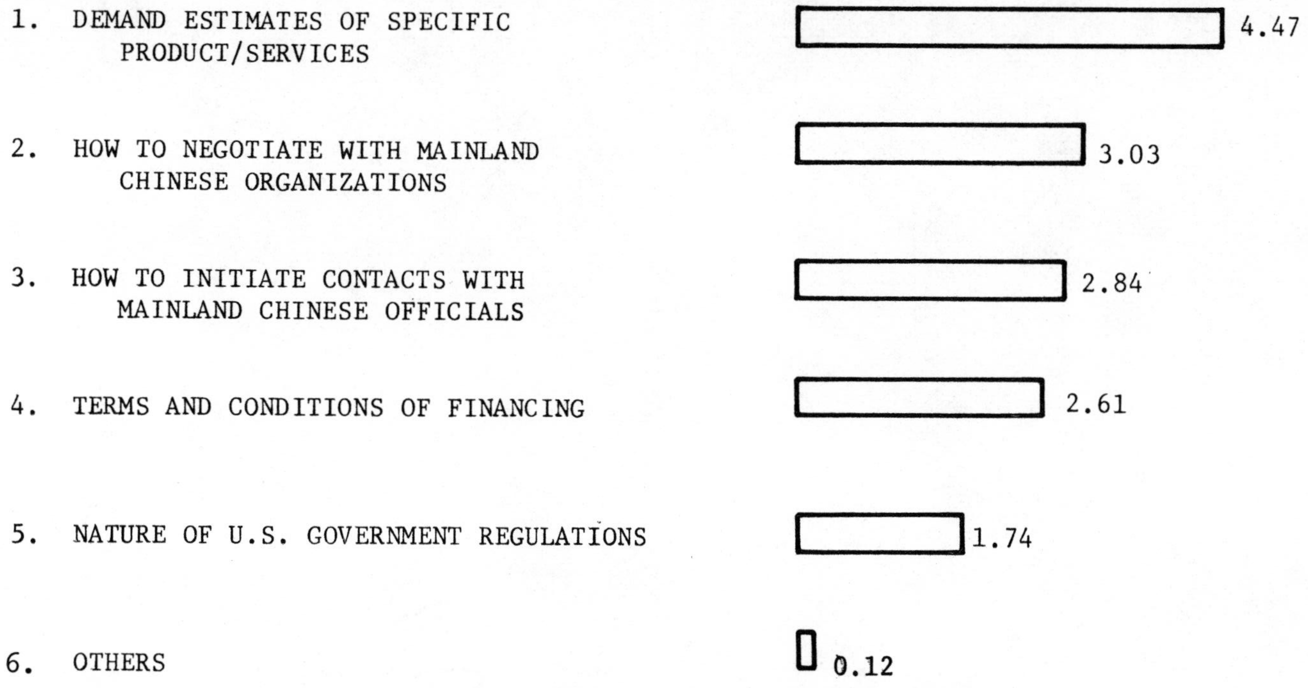

1. DEMAND ESTIMATES OF SPECIFIC
   PRODUCT/SERVICES   4.47

2. HOW TO NEGOTIATE WITH MAINLAND
   CHINESE ORGANIZATIONS   3.03

3. HOW TO INITIATE CONTACTS WITH
   MAINLAND CHINESE OFFICIALS   2.84

4. TERMS AND CONDITIONS OF FINANCING   2.61

5. NATURE OF U.S. GOVERNMENT REGULATIONS   1.74

6. OTHERS   0.12

and Eastern European countries. This will be particularly true with large sales of machinery; PRC officials will be especially anxious to secure the best possible terms of financing. The availability of some form of assistance from the U.S. government in the form of loan-guarantee financing and other means will play a critical role.

Information about U.S. government regulations on trade with the PRC is viewed as relatively less important, because American companies are able to secure the necessary information and interpretation from appropriate agencies of the U.S. government concerned with matters of trade with Communist countries. In addition, the Department of Commerce has released a growing body of information on regulations pertaining to trade with the PRC.

Under the "other" category the primary question raised was the effect of a company's trade with Taiwan on its trade with the PRC.

PENETRATING PRC MARKETS

Methods. The methods of foreign-market penetration include exports, licensing arrangements, investments (joint ventures, wholly-owned subsidiaries), and other forms such as production-sharing agreements* and turnkey projects.**

---

*Under production-sharing agreements, the foreign company provides the necessary imported materials (know-how, equipment) for a project while an indigenous organization provides the remainder. The foreign company receives its payments in the form of, or part of, the production. The benefit of such an arrangement is that the host country receives the necessary foreign resources without expenditure of foreign exchange while the foreign company is able to secure products at a lower cost than if they were manufactured in its own country. For example, several Western companies have established such arrangements with Eastern European countries.

**Turnkey projects refer to a contractual relationship between a foreign company and an indigenous private or public organization to establish a complete project, train nationals, and offer assurances that the project will function at a given level of rated capacity. Once the project is operational, the foreign company withdraws.

Graph 50 presents the response to the question of methods of penetrating PRC markets. Both at present and in five years, by far the most frequent method is export. This is a relatively simple method and involves fewer risks. Licensing is the second most frequently stated method, but it entails a higher level of commitment and risks for the foreign company. Production-sharing arrangements are relatively unimportant compared to the first two methods, both at present and in five years, which is largely due to limited know-how by American companies interested in doing business in the PRC and uncertainty which still characterizes the relationship between the U.S. and PRC. Turnkey projects are ranked the lowest both at present and in five years-- because of the greater risks inherent in such projects especially in the light of the limited knowledge of PRC markets by American companies.

In brief, American companies propose to concentrate on the relatively safer forms--exporting and licensing--to penetrate PRC markets. During the next five years, executives do not foresee entering into more risky types of ventures, and this is consistent with the pattern preferred by American companies in other Communist countries such as the Soviet Union and Eastern Europe. (In fact, American companies have preferred export in penetrating non-Communist countries as well. Host-country restrictions have forced companies to use other methods.)

Sources of Penetration. Through what organizations--U.S.-based, foreign affiliates in Asia and elsewhere, external organizations (trading companies), individuals (overseas Chinese community in Southeast Asia)-- are American companies likely to penetrate PRC markets? Of course, companies will use a combination of organizations at any moment in time, and the choice will depend on the company's knowledge of the PRC, avail-

GRAPH 50

RANKING OF METHODS FOR PENETRATING PRC MARKETS

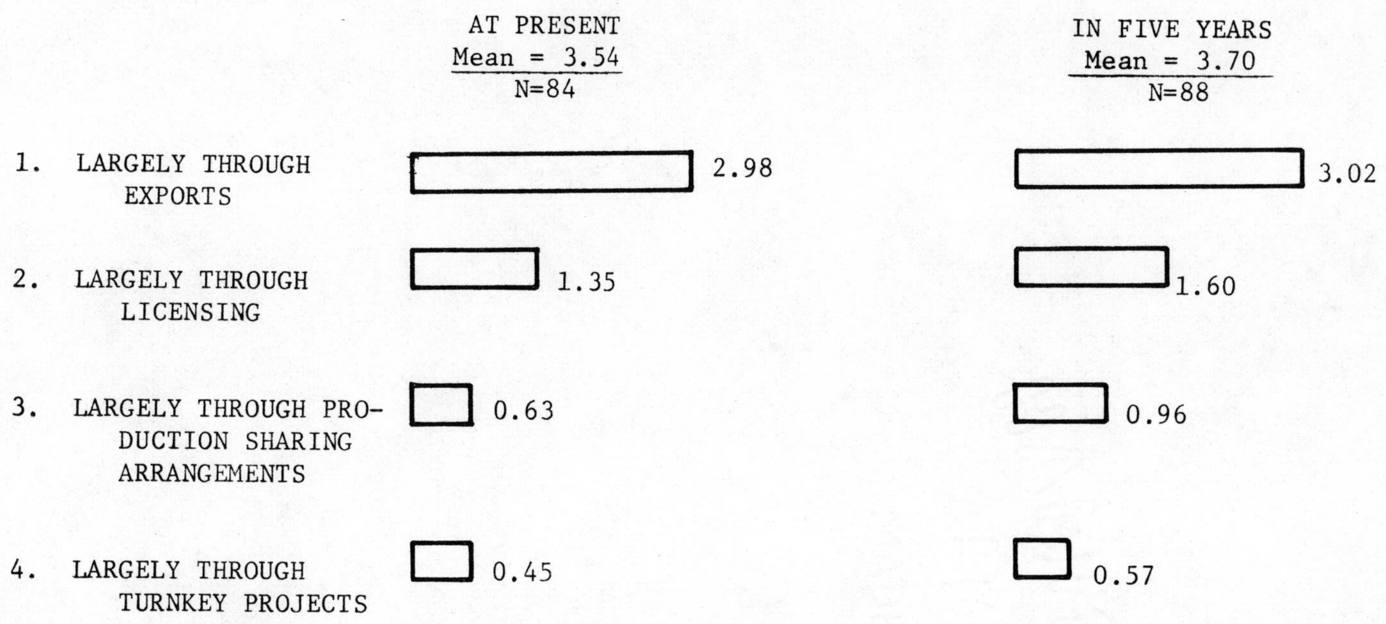

AT PRESENT
Mean = 3.54
N=84

IN FIVE YEARS
Mean = 3.70
N=88

1. LARGELY THROUGH EXPORTS — 2.98 / 3.02

2. LARGELY THROUGH LICENSING — 1.35 / 1.60

3. LARGELY THROUGH PRODUCTION SHARING ARRANGEMENTS — 0.63 / 0.96

4. LARGELY THROUGH TURNKEY PROJECTS — 0.45 / 0.57

ability of informed and dependable individuals outside of the organization, and preferences on the part of the PRC.

Graph 51 presents the response. At present, trading companies are most frequently preferred because of their greater knowledge and contacts in the PRC which could lead to the proper introductions for a company. The parent company in the U.S. is the second most frequently stated source, indicating that companies plan to continue their direct explorations with the PRC while using trading companies. Asian affiliates are the third most frequently mentioned category. Their geographical proximity and perhaps greater access to knowledgeable organizations and individuals adds to their importance in a company's overall strategy for entering the PRC markets. European affiliates rank fourth, particularly in countries such as the United Kingdom and West Germany which already do a significant volume of trade with the PRC. Japanese affiliates rank fifth. The latter observation is somewhat surprising because Japan is the largest non-Communist trading partner of PRC. However, other considerations might suggest why American companies assign relatively low importance to Japanese affiliates. At present, restrictions on extent of foreign ownership in Japan limit American companies to a minority ownership position in most cases. Exports from Japan are made from the joint venture company which offers the Japanese partners 50% of the profits. American companies might be concerned that their Japanese partners could end up controlling the joint venture exports to the PRC. Canadian affiliates rank relatively low because of the emergence of other countries with equal if not better relations with the PRC. The overseas Chinese community in Southeast Asia has a complex network of contacts within the region and with the PRC, but companies assign limited importance to this source because of

GRAPH 51

RANKING OF SOURCES IN PENETRATING PRC MARKETS

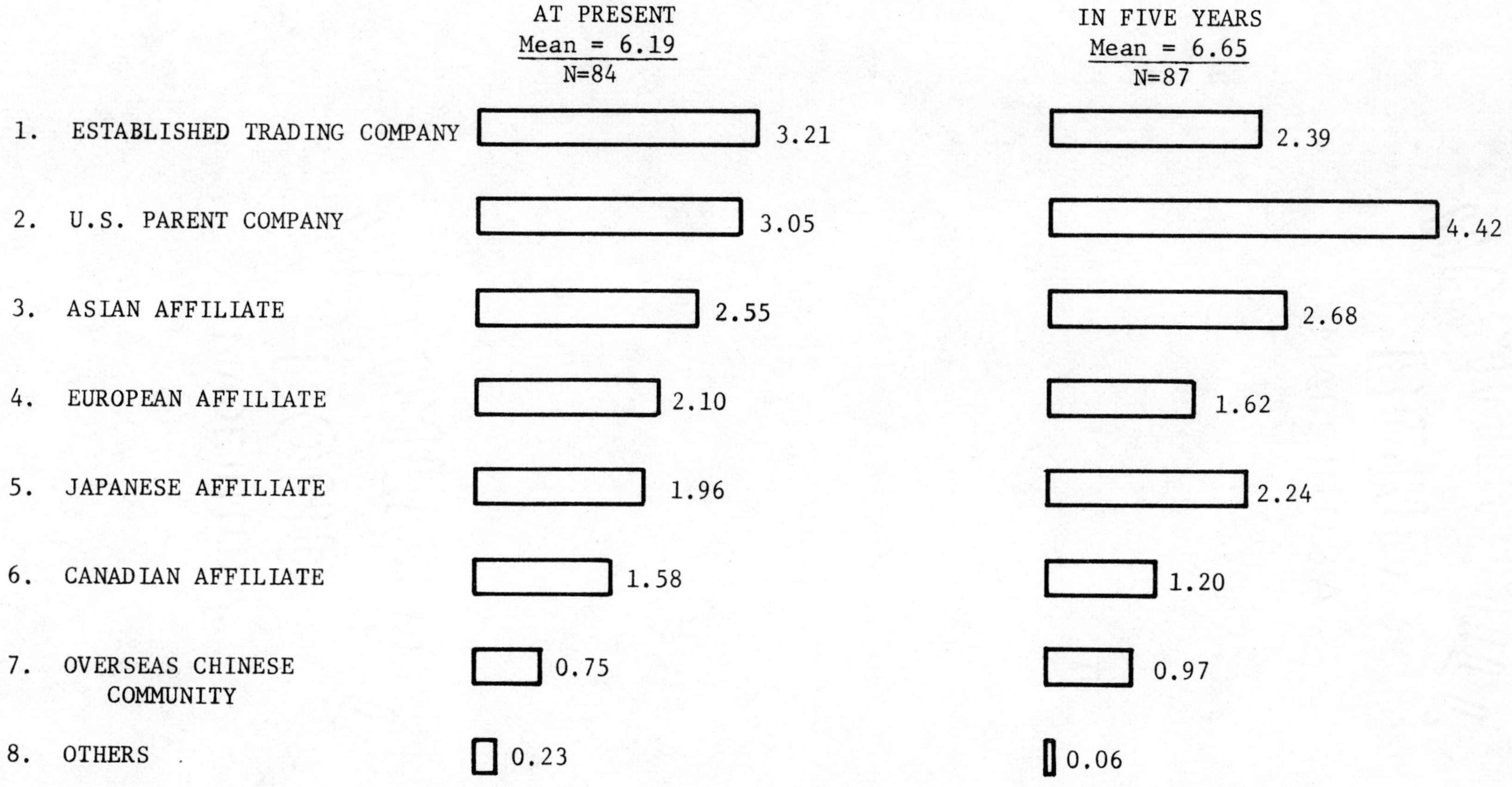

AT PRESENT
Mean = 6.19
N=84

IN FIVE YEARS
Mean = 6.65
N=87

1. ESTABLISHED TRADING COMPANY — 3.21 / 2.39
2. U.S. PARENT COMPANY — 3.05 / 4.42
3. ASIAN AFFILIATE — 2.55 / 2.68
4. EUROPEAN AFFILIATE — 2.10 / 1.62
5. JAPANESE AFFILIATE — 1.96 / 2.24
6. CANADIAN AFFILIATE — 1.58 / 1.20
7. OVERSEAS CHINESE COMMUNITY — 0.75 / 0.97
8. OTHERS — 0.23 / 0.06

the uncertain status of such Chinese in the PRC, and the (probable) preference of PRC officials to deal directly with Americans.

The sources which companies expect to use in five years to penetrate PRC markets show rankings different from those at present. Thus, by far the most important source in five years will be the U.S. parent company. During the next five years companies obviously hope to increase their know-how in dealing with the PRC, and top management probably expects the level of difficulties or the volume of trade to be such that these should be concentrated in the hands of the parent company.

The second most frequent source will be the Asian affiliate, followed by trading companies and Japanese affiliate (the last increasing in importance in five years). European affiliates are expected to decline in importance while the Canadian, overseas Chinese, and "others" will remain largely at their current levels.

COMPETITION

As with American companies, companies in other countries are aware of the potential of the markets of the PRC. However, many other developed countries have greater experience in doing business with the PRC and at present are more welcome to the PRC because, for instance, of their acceptable political viewpoint on Vietnam. U.S. companies, relative newcomers to PRC markets and the methods of doing business there, are thus facing stiff competition.

What are the major sources of competition and how are they ranked in terms of importance by American companies? Graph 52 presents the response.

Japan, presently by far the leading source of competition for

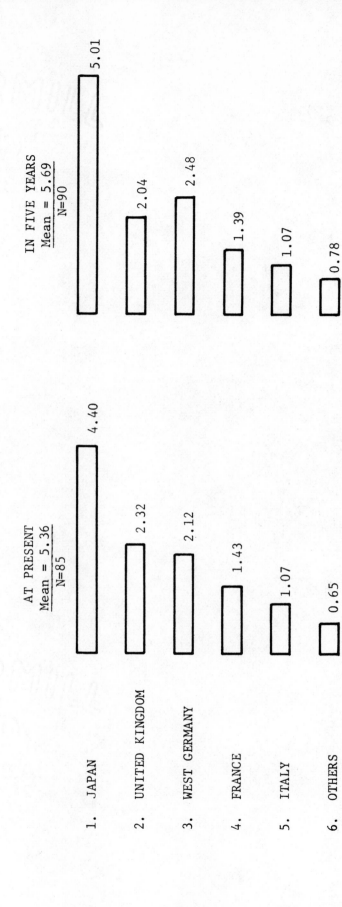

GRAPH 52

MAJOR SOURCES OF COMPETITION FOR PRC MARKETS,
AT PRESENT AND IN FIVE YEARS

American companies, is the largest foreign trading partner with the PRC. As with the other Asian countries, Japanese companies have been successful in the PRC largely because they are competitive on the basis of price and technology. The other sources of competition in decreasing order of importance are the United Kingdom, West Germany, France, and Italy.

The picture changes in five years. Thus, Japan becomes yet an even stronger competitor. Extension of diplomatic recognition to the PRC will, of course, further strengthen the hands of the Japanese in the PRC. Also, the Japanese will continue to be attracted to the PRC primarily because they are competitive on the basis of price and technology and need markets for their manufactures, as well as access to raw materials. The other change in ranking of competition occurs for West Germany, which moves from third to second position, thereby displacing the United Kingdom.

OBSERVATIONS

At this stage, many American companies simply do not know what their policies or programs of action are likely to be toward the People's Republic of China. The expectations of companies presented in the foregoing pages are based on limited information and knowledge of PRC markets and of the requirements of doing business there. Policies and programs of action based on greater knowledge and experience will emerge over the coming months and years and will necessitate modifications or outright reversals of policies which companies contemplate pursuing at this time.

Nevertheless, the expectations of American companies permit some general observations on the nature and characteristics of trade with the PRC:

1) As PRC markets gain in importance, they will play a greater role in overall planning by a company in terms of its Asian and global operations.

2) There is obviously a potential market in the PRC. The main question is of converting this potential into reality in the form of concrete sales. As with the Soviet Union and Eastern European countries, American companies will encounter difficulties in achieving such a conversion in the PRC, and it is unlikely that a large volume of sales will be generated in the short-term.

3) During the past year, many companies have built high expectations about what they can do in the PRC markets. More often than not such expectations are based on limited information and knowledge of the realities of doing business with the PRC. As companies explore specific business proposals, they will recognize the range of difficulties in doing business with the PRC, and this will result in a "deflation" of expectations. As a result, companies with a short-term outlook toward the PRC and with limited maturity in international business will most probably fade away, leaving the field to the more experienced international companies.

4) The extent of U.S. exports to the PRC will be related to the extent of PRC exports to the U.S. Still, a major question is whether the Chinese will be able to offer goods and services with a market in the U.S. Companies might consider shifting their purchases of certain types of goods from other countries to the PRC in the hope of gaining

greater access to the PRC markets. But what will be the implications of such a move for the countries losing exports, especially when all developing countries including those in Asia are emphasizing exports? Also, should companies remain with tried and proven sources of supply instead of shifting to the PRC? It is highly unlikely that companies will undertake such transfers in the short-term, but when such transfers are made they will have serious implications for other developing countries, particularly those in Asia.

*   *   *   *

In brief, the China market is potentially large and therefore important. Multinational enterprises simply cannot afford to ignore such a market any more than they can ignore the markets of a country like India. Yet, effective cultivation of PRC markets will require a sustained interest based on a realistic understanding of the characteristics inherent in doing business with the PRC. And, of course, it is not unlikely that the geo-political forces which have encouraged a rapprochement between the U.S. and the PRC will change for the worse or for the better. In either case, uncertainty will remain a central feature of U.S.-PRC trade for some time to come.

Bibliography

Books

Adams, T. F. M., and N. Kobayashi. *The World of Japanese Business*. Tokyo: Kodansha International, 1970.

Abegglen, James C. *Business Strategies for Japan*. Tokyo: Sophia University Press, 1970.

Allan, David E. (ed.). *Asian Contract Law: A Survey of Current Problems*. Melbourne: Melbourne University Press, 1969.

Almond, Gabriel A., and James C. Coleman (eds.). *The Politics of the Developing Areas*. Princeton: Princeton University Press, 1960.

Asian Development Bank. *Southeast Asia's Economy in the 1970s*. New York: Frederick A. Praeger, 1971.

Ballon, Robert J. *Doing Business in Japan*. Rutland, Vermont: Charles Tuttle, 1968.

------. *Joint Ventures in Japan*. Rutland, Vermont: Charles Tuttle, 1967.

Baranson, J. *Manufacturing Problems in India*. Syracuse: Syracuse University Press, 1967.

Barnett, Doak, A. and Edwin C. Reischauer (eds.). *United States and China: The Next Decade*. New York: Frederick A. Praeger, 1970.

Duncan, James S. *A Businessman Looks at Red China*. Princeton: Van Nostrand, 1965.

Eckstein, Alexander (ed.). *China Trade Prospects and U.S. Policy*. New York: Frederick A. Praeger, 1971.

Emery, F. *The Financial Institutions of Southeast Asia: A Country-by-Country Study*. New York: Frederick A. Praeger, 1970.

Golay, Frank H. (ed.). *Underdevelopment and Economic Nationalism in Southeast Asia*. Ithaca: Cornell University Press, 1969.

Herbert, Jean. *An Introduction to Asia*. George Allen and Unwin Ltd., 1960.

Kapoor, Ashok. *International Business Negotiations: A Study in India*. New York: New York University Press, 1970.

-----, and Robert McKay. *Managing International Markets: A Survey of Training Practices and Emerging Trends.* Princeton: The Darwin Press, 1971.

-----, and Phillip D. Grub (eds.). *The Multinational Enterprise in Transition: Selected Readings and Essays.* Princeton: The Darwin Press, 1972.

-----, J. Boddewyn, *et.al. World Business Systems and Environments.* Scranton, Pa.: Intext, 1972.

-----, and Jean Boddewyn. *International Business-Government Relations: The U.S. Corporate Experience.* New York: American Management Association, forthcoming.

Kahin, George McT. *Major Governments of Asia.* Ithaca: Cornell University Press, 1963.

Kerr, Clark, *et.al. Industrialization and Industrial Man.* New York: Oxford University Press, 1966.

Kidron, Michael. *Foreign Investment in India.* New York: Oxford University Press, 1966.

Kojima, Kiyoshi. *Japan and a Pacific Free Trade Area.* Tokyo: University of Tokyo Press, 1971.

Lockwood, W. W. *The State and Economic Enterprise in Japan.* Princeton: Princeton University Press, 1965.

Morley, James W. (ed.). *Forecast for Japan: Security in the 1970s.* Princeton: Princeton University Press, 1972.

Purcell, Victor. *The Chinese in Southeast Asia.* London: Oxford University Press, 1965.

Richman, Barry M. *Industrial Society in Communist China.* New York: Random House, 1969.

Suyin, Han. *China in the Year 2001.* New York: Basic Books, 1967.

Tilman, R. *Man, State and Society in Contemporary Southeast Asia.* New York: Frederick A. Praeger, 1969.

U.S. Congress Joint Economic Committee. *An Economic Profile of Mainland China.* New York: Frederick A. Praeger, 1969.

Yanaga, Chitoshi. *Big Business in Japanese Politics.* New Haven: Yale University Press, 1968.

Yoshino, M. *Japan's Managerial System.* Cambridge: M.I.T. Press, 1968.

-----. *The Japanese Marketing System.* Cambridge: M.I.T. Press, 1971.

Journals and Periodicals

Economic Bulletin for Asia and the Far East

Economic Survey of Asia and the Far East

The Economic Weekly, Bombay, India

The Far Eastern Economic Review, Hong Kong

The Oriental Economist, Tokyo, Japan

APPENDIX A

Indicators of Market Size--Asia

	Population [A,L]			GNP [A,C,E,L,N]		National Income [A,C,E,L,N]			Manufacturing as % of domestic product [L,N]		Exchange rate [A,C,G,L]
	Total 1970 (million)	% 5-year increase	1975 forecast (million)	Total 1970 ($ billion)	% 5-year increase constant prices	Total 1970 ($ billion)	% 5-year increase current prices	Per capita 1970 ($)	1969	1964	Local currency per US $ July 31, 1971
ASIA											
Afghanistan	17.1	13.8	19.3	1.00 [1]	18.0	0.87	68.0	64	3	2	45.0000
Burma	27.6	11.5	31.2	1.80 [1]	1.3	1.53	1.5	56	10	9	4,7620
Cambodia**	6.8	11.5	8.3	0.84	14.6	0.71	22.0	104	12	18	55.5400
Ceylon	12.5	12.1	14.2	2.12	27.9	1.85	58.3	148	12	9	5.958
China	750.0	7.9	825.8	65.00	23.1	55.00	25.2	74	27	25	2.4600
Hong Kong	4.3	16.2	4.7	3.30	63.5	2.80	83.3	667	71	69	6.0600
India	550.4	13.1	632.5	47.91 [1]	13.4	46.14	67.8	84	16	16	7.4600
Indonesia	115.0	9.6	140.3	8.68	13.4 [3]	7.88	66.2 [3]	69	10	8	340.0000
Japan	103.5	5.7	109.9	196.06	66.5	156.83	122.6	1,515	36	32	357.4000
Korea, North	13.9	14.8	15.9	3.01	50.0	2.54	65.0	180	25	23	2.5700
Korea, South	31.8	12.0	36.2	8.20	72.5	7.00	217.9	220	24	20	370.0000
Laos	3.0	12.5	3.4	0.36	33.8	0.31	36.4	105	5	5	240.0000
Malaysia	10.9	16.0	12.4	3.86	34.6	3.74	37.0	342	12	10	3.0600
Nepal	11.0	8.9	12.6	0.84	13.5	0.70	39.0	63	2	2	10.1250
Pakistan	114.2	11.0	162.4	16.90	32.4	14.68	64.6	129	12	11	4.7340
Philippines+	36.7	13.3	45.3	6.16	28.2	5.10	88.0	139	17	18	3.9000
Ryukyus	1.0	8.6	1.1	0.84	56.2	0.74	118.0	733	10	10	1.0000
Singapore	2.1	10.2	2.4	1.82	61.0	1.55	82.9	756	14	9	3.0600
Taiwan	14.0	12.9	15.6	5.44	62.4	4.26	86.1	303	23	21	40.1000
Thailand	35.8	16.5	42.6	6.76	52.6	5.54	66.9	155	15	13	21,0000
Vietnam, North	21.2	11.3	23.4	2.01	15.9	1.71	27.6	81	12	10	3.5000
Vietnam, South+	18.3	13.7	19.8	6.42	30.9	5.46	477.5	298	11	9	275.00
TOTAL ASIA	1901.1		2237.5	389.33		326.94		172			

	Total exports [C,F,L]		Total imports [C,F,L]		Imports from US [D,F,L,M]		Imports from EEC [B,F]		International liquidity [C]
	1970 f.o.b. ($ million)	% 5-year increase	1970 c.i.f. ($ million)	% 5-year increase	1970 f.o.b. ($ million)	% 5-year increase	1970 f.o.b. ($ million)	% 5-year increase	Total reserves June 1971 ($ million)
ASIA									
Afghanistan	—	—	—	—	10	—26	—	—	45
Burma	106	—53	162	—34	11	—18	—	—	59
Cambodia**	63	—40	77	—25	2	35	—	—	—
Ceylon	342	—16	389	25	12	23	38	3	53
China	2060	11	2165	28	—	—	349	50	—
Hong Kong	2514	120	2905	85	399	109	278	103	—
India	2027	20	2124	—25	572	—38	282	-33	1126
Indonesia	811	15	883	27	263	—	185	34	—
Japan	19333	129	18896	131	4610	121	986	188	7800
Korea, North	—	—	—	—	—	—	—	—	—
Korea, South	835	377	1984	329	636	132	126	—	581
Laos	3	200	128	374	8	—3	—	—	—
Malaysia	1680	36	1396	27	66	—27	119	—20	835
Nepal	79	—	113	—	1	—17	—	—	102
Pakistan	723	37	1151	10	325	—3	210	4	215
Philippines+	1062	38	1210	35	370	6	144	69	299
Ryukyus	—	—	—	—	42	1	—	—	—
Singapore	1554	58	2461	98	239	—	164	—	317
Taiwan	1428	217	1524	174	526	125	97	246	564
Thailand	697	12	1292	76	150	39	162	51	934
Vietnam, North	—	—	—	—	—	—	—	—	—
Vietnam, South	11	—69	550	68	352	85	66	43	203
TOTAL ASIA									

Reprinted from the 1972 reprint edition of "Indicators of
Market Size in 130 Countries," with the permission of the
publisher, Business International Corporation (New York).

Source: (A) UN Monthly Bulletin of Statistics. (B) OECD Commodity Trade Statistics-Series A. (C) International Financial Statistics (IMF). (D) U.S. Department of Commerce. (E) Agency for International Development. (F) Direction of Trade (IMF). (G) Pick's Currency Yearbook. (H) Jan. 1970 data revised by U.S. Department of Commerce, as reported in The World Automotive Market 1971, Johnston International Publishing Corp. (I) The World's Telephones, American Telephone & Telegraph Co. (J) 1971 World Radio-TV Handbook. (K) 1970 UN Statistical Yearbook. (L) BI unpublished data. (M) UN Commodity Trade Statistics-Series D. (N) UN Yearbook of National Accounts Statistics.

Footnotes: (**) Devalued during 1969. (+) Devalued during 1970. (1) Fiscal year. (3) 1968-70. (4) March 1971.

APPENDIX B

Questionnaire--Asia

QUESTIONNAIRE--ASIA

BACKGROUND INFORMATION

1) Please list the two or three major products in which your company
is engaged?

_____

2) What was your company's annual sales volume last year? Please check.

_____Less than $200 million   _____$600-1000 million

_____$200-300 million   _____$1001-2000 million

_____$301-600 million   _____Over $2000 million

3) What percent of your company's annual sales and profits for last year
were derived from all overseas and from Asian operations? Please check
the appropriate percentage range.

a. Derived from all overseas operations:

	0-5%	5-10%	11-25%	26-50%	51-75%	Over 75%
as a percent of annual sales	___	___	___	___	___	___
as a percent of annual profits	___	___	___	___	___	___

b. Derived from Asian operations:

	0-1%	1-2%	2-3%	3-6%	6-15%	Over 15%
as a percent of annual sales	___	___	___	___	___	___
as a percent of annual profits	___	___	___	___	___	___

4) In which of the following Asian countries does your company have
operations? Please check.

_____Japan   _____Taiwan   _____Indonesia   _____Malaysia

_____S. Korea   _____Philippines   _____Thailand   _____India

181

5) What type(s) of operation(s) does your company have in each country? Please check.

	Japan	S. Korea	Taiwan	Philippines	Indonesia	Thailand	Malaysia	India
Manufacture Largely for Export	___	___	___	___	___	___	___	___
Manufacture Largely for Host Country	___	___	___	___	___	___	___	___
Management Services Contracts	___	___	___	___	___	___	___	___
Distributorship	___	___	___	___	___	___	___	___
Sales Office	___	___	___	___	___	___	___	___
License Agreement	___	___	___	___	___	___	___	___
Other (Please Specify)	___	___	___	___	___	___	___	___

ATTITUDE OF ASIAN GOVERNMENTS

6) a. In your opinion, how stable are the present governments for each of the following Asian countries. Please check.

	Japan	S. Korea	Taiwan	Philippines	Indonesia	Thailand	Malaysia	India
Highly Stable	___	___	___	___	___	___	___	___
Stable	___	___	___	___	___	___	___	___
Moderately Stable	___	___	___	___	___	___	___	___
Moderately Unstable	___	___	___	___	___	___	___	___
Unstable	___	___	___	___	___	___	___	___
Highly Unstable	___	___	___	___	___	___	___	___

b. In your opinion, how <u>stable</u> are the governments for each of the following Asian countries likely to be <u>in five years</u>? Please check.

	Japan	S. Korea	Taiwan	Philip- pines	Indo- nesia	Thai- land	Malay- sia	India
Highly Stable	___	___	___	___	___	___	___	___
Stable	___	___	___	___	___	___	___	___
Moderately Stable	___	___	___	___	___	___	___	___
Moderately Unstable	___	___	___	___	___	___	___	___
Unstable	___	___	___	___	___	___	___	___
Highly Unstable	___	___	___	___	___	___	___	___

c. What are the <u>main</u> <u>reasons</u> for your response in 6 b above? Please check.

	Japan	S. Korea	Taiwan	Philip- pines	Indo- nesia	Thai- land	Malay- sia	India
Increasing Strength of Political Op- position Groups	___	___	___	___	___	___	___	___
Increasing Social Unrest	___	___	___	___	___	___	___	___
Greater Sense of National Unity	___	___	___	___	___	___	___	___
Economic Stabili- ty	___	___	___	___	___	___	___	___
Consolidation of Power by Poli- tical Leaders	___	___	___	___	___	___	___	___
Other (Please Specify)	___	___	___	___	___	___	___	___

7) a. In your opinion, what is the present attitude of each of the following Asian governments toward the following types of direct foreign investment? Place the appropriate number in the space:

Strong Encouragement   = 1
Moderate Encouragement   = 2
Moderate Restrictiveness = 3
Strong Restrictiveness   = 4
No Clear-cut Attutide   = 5

	Japan	S. Korea	Taiwan	Philippines	Indonesia	Thailand	Malaysia	India
Manufacture Largely for Export								
Manufacture Largely for Host-Country Market								
Extractive Industries								
Management Services Contracts								
Technology-Intensive Investments								
Labor-Intensive Investments								

b. In your opinion, what will be the attitude of each of the following Asian governments in five years toward the following types of direct foreign investment? Place the appropriate number in the space:

Strong Encouragement   = 1
Moderate Encouragement   = 2
Moderate Restrictiveness = 3
Strong Restrictiveness   = 4
No Clear-cut Attitude
    Discernible   = 5

	Japan	S. Korea	Taiwan	Philip- pines	Indo- nesia	Thai- land	Malay- sia	India
Manufacture Largely for Export	___	___	___	___	___	___	___	___
Manufacture Largely for Host-Country Market	___	___	___	___	___	___	___	___
Extractive Industries	___	___	___	___	___	___	___	___
Management Services Contracts	___	___	___	___	___	___	___	___
Technology-Intensive Investments	___	___	___	___	___	___	___	___
Labor-Intensive Investments	___	___	___	___	___	___	___	___

8) a. In your opinion, what is the present attitude of each of the following Asian governments toward extent of foreign ownership of investments like yours? Please check.

	Japan	S. Korea	Taiwan	Philip- pines	Indo- nesia	Thai- land	Malay- sia	India
100% Ownership Permitted	___	___	___	___	___	___	___	___
Majority Ownership Permitted	___	___	___	___	___	___	___	___
Only 50-50 Owner- ship Permitted	___	___	___	___	___	___	___	___
Only Minority Ownership Permitted	___	___	___	___	___	___	___	___
No Foreign Owner- ship Permitted	___	___	___	___	___	___	___	___
Initial Ownership Unrestricted, but Total Divest- ment Required over Time	___	___	___	___	___	___	___	___
No Policy Discern- able	___	___	___	___	___	___	___	___

b. In your opinion, <u>what will be</u> the <u>attitude</u> of each of the following Asian governments <u>toward extent of foreign ownership</u> <u>in five years</u> for investments like yours?

	Japan	S. Korea	Taiwan	Philip- pines	Indo- nesia	Thai- land	Malay- sia	India
100% Ownership Permitted	___	___	___	___	___	___	___	___
Majority Ownership Permitted	___	___	___	___	___	___	___	___
Only 50-50 Owner- ship Permitted	___	___	___	___	___	___	___	___
Only Minority Owner- ship Permitted	___	___	___	___	___	___	___	___
No Foreign Ownership Permitted	___	___	___	___	___	___	___	___
Initial Ownership Unrestricted, but Total Divestment Required Over Time	___	___	___	___	___	___	___	___
No Policy Discern- able	___	___	___	___	___	___	___	___

c. What are the major reasons for your response in 8b above? Please check.

	Japan	S. Korea	Taiwan	Philip- pines	Indo- nesia	Thai- land	Malay- sia	India
Economic Growth	___	___	___	___	___	___	___	___
Greater Foreign Ex- change Problems	___	___	___	___	___	___	___	___
Greater Need for For- eign Managerial Skill and/or Technology	___	___	___	___	___	___	___	___
Greater Pressure by Local Businessmen	___	___	___	___	___	___	___	___
Reduced Foreign Ex- change Problems	___	___	___	___	___	___	___	___

8 c continued next page

	Japan	S. Korea	Taiwan	Philip- pines	Indo- nesia	Thai- land	Malay- sia	India
Greater Role of Government as a Partner in Industrial Projects								
Other (Please Specify)								

9) a. In your opinion, how strong is the pressure of each of the following Asian governments to staff all top management positions (e.g., President, Comptroller) with host-country nationals? Please check.

	Japan	S. Korea	Taiwan	Philip- pines	Indo- nesia	Thai- land	Malay- sia	India
No Pressure								
Slight Pressure, but No Deadline								
Moderate Pressure with Deadline of Over Five Years								
Moderate Pressure with Deadline within Five Years								
Strong Pressure with Fixed Deadline of Within Five Years								
Other (Please Specify)								

b. In your opinion, what top expatriate management personnel will your company tend to withdraw first from its overseas operations? Place 1 for first to be withdrawn, a 2 for second to be withdrawn, and so on, in the space provided.

_____President   _____Marketing Manager   _____Financial Manager

_____Plant, Production and/or Technical Manager   _____Other (Please Specify)

187

10) a. In your opinion, what <u>level of difficulty</u> are each of the <u>obstacles</u> listed below likely to cause in <u>present</u> everyday operations like yours in each of the following countries? Place the appropriate number in the space:

Acceptable Level of Difficulties = 1
Major Difficulties = 2
Severely Handicapping = 3

	Japan	S. Korea	Taiwan	Philip- pines	Indo- nesia	Thai- land	Malay- sia	India
Increasing Local Con- tent Requirement								
Currency Instability								
Restrictive Earnings Remittance Policy								
Unrealistic Price Controls								
Import Restrictions								
Other (Please Specify)								

b. In your opinion, what will be the <u>level of difficulty</u> each of the <u>obstacles</u> listed below is likely to cause everyday operations like yours in each of the following countries <u>in five years</u>? Place the appropriate number in the space:

Acceptable Level of Difficulties = 1
Major Difficulties = 2
Severely Handicapping = 3

	Japan	S. Korea	Taiwan	Philip- pines	Indo- nesia	Thai- land	Malay- sia	India
Increasing Local Con- tent Requirements								
Currency Instability								
Restrictive Earnings Remittance Policy								
Unrealistic Price Controls								
Import Restrictions								
Other (Please Specify)								

11) What was the time it took to secure approval from the host government once you had decided to go ahead with the project for your last investment in each country where you have investments? Please check.

	Japan	S. Korea	Taiwan	Philippines	Indonesia	Thailand	Malaysia	India
Less than 3 Months								
3 to 7 Months								
7 Months to 1 Year								
1 to 2 Years								
Over 2 Years								

ATTITUDE OF AMERICAN COMPANIES

12) a. What is your company's policy on extent of ownership of investments in Asia? Please check.

_____ 1-100% Ownership

_____ 2-Majority ownership with wide distribution of shares to nationals

_____ 3-Majority ownership with specified local groups

_____ 4-Minority ownership with wide distribution of shares to nationals

_____ 5-Minority ownership with specified local groups

_____ 6-Initial majority ownership reduced over time to minority position

_____ 7-Majority ownership with host government as a partner

_____ 8-Minority ownership with host government as a partner

_____ 9-Other (Please Specify) _____

b. Which of the above numbered (1-9) ownership configurations best represent the ownership configuration of your Asian operations today and what you expect them to be in five years? Place the appropriate number from 12 a above in the space for each country in which you have investments.

189

	Japan	S. Korea	Taiwan	Philip-pines	Indo-nesia	Thai-land	Malay-sia	India
Today								
In Five Years								

13) In which Asian country(ies) is your company likely to make new and/or additional investments over the next five years? Please check.

_____ Japan   _____ Taiwan   _____ Indonesia   _____ Malaysia

_____ S. Korea   _____ Philippines   _____ Thailand   _____ India

14) What types of investments is your company likely to make in each of those countries? Please check.

	Japan	S. Korea	Taiwan	Philip-pines	Indo-nesia	Thai-land	Malay-sia	India
Manufacture Largely for Export								
Manufacture Largely for Host Country Market								
Extractive Indus-tries								
Management Services Contracts								
Distributorship								
License Agreement								
Other (Please Specify)								

15) In your opinion, to what extent are your company's investments in Asia likely to change (increase or decrease) over the next five years? Please check.

	0-10%	11-25%	26-50%	51-75%	Over 75%
Increase by					
Decrease by					

_____ Remain at the present level

190

16) In your opinion, what are the key objectives of your company's investments in Asia. Please check the key objective(s) for each of your Asian investments by country.

	Japan	S. Korea	Taiwan	Philippines	Indonesia	Thailand	Malaysia	India
Promote Export of U.S. Raw Materials and Semi-finished Goods								
Promote Export of U.S. Machinery and Equipment								
Import Restrictions								
Develop New Markets								
Obtain Raw Materials								
Export to Third Countries								
Export to the U.S.								
Dividends, Royalties								
Other (Please Specify)								

JAPANESE COMPETITION

17) a. What is the extent of competition by Japanese companies at present and how competitive do you expect them to be in five years? Please check.

	At Present	In Five Years
No Competition		
Limited Competition		
Growing Competition		
Extremely Strong Competition		

191

b. What are the <u>advantages</u> Japanese companies have over American companies in doing business in Asia <u>at present</u> and <u>in five years</u>? Please check.

	At Present	In Five Years
They possess greater knowledge of Asian customs	_____	_____
They are Asians	_____	_____
They are less ethical in business dealings	_____	_____
Asia is a very important market for Japanese companies	_____	_____
Japanese government offers important assistance to Japanese companies	_____	_____
Japanese are competitive in price and/or technology	_____	_____

<u>Thank you very much</u> for your help in this project. We would be interested in learning your <u>firm's name</u> and <u>your title</u> although these two items are completely <u>optional</u>.

Firm's Name: _____

Respondent's Title: _____

If you are interested in learning of the findings of this study, we will gladly send you a copy of the results when available. Please indicate to whom they should be sent.

Name: _____

Address: _____

_____

_____

APPENDIX C

Questionnaire—Mainland China

THE AMERICAN BUSINESSMAN AND MAINLAND CHINA'S MARKETS: PROBLEMS AND PROSPECTS IN THE 1970s

I

1. What was your company's <u>annual sales volume last year</u>? Please check.

    _____Less than $200 million   _____$601-1000 million

    _____$200-300 million   _____$1001-2000 million

    _____$301-600 million   _____over $2000 million

2. Please list two or three of your company's <u>major products</u> or <u>services</u> which are likely to have a market <u>in Mainland China</u>?

    _____

    _____

II

3. How would you define your company's <u>interest</u> at <u>present</u> and <u>in five years</u> in Mainland China's markets?

	At present	In five years
Very strong interest	_____	_____
Strong interest	_____	_____
Limited interest	_____	_____
No interest	_____	_____

194

4. What are the main reasons for the level of your company's interest at present and why is it likely to change over the next five years? Please rank 1, 2, 3 etc. in order of importance.

	At present	In five years
Relaxation of U.S. government restrictions	_____	_____
Potentially large market	_____	_____
Considerable demand at present	_____	_____
To keep up with moves of competitors	_____	_____
Small size of actual and potential market	_____	_____
More profitable opportunities in other countries	_____	_____
Many unknowns in doing business with Mainland China	_____	_____

III

5. What are the main sources of information on Mainland China's markets used by your company? Please rank 1, 2, 3 in order of importance.

_____In-house studies

_____Individual consultants

_____Experienced trading companies

_____U.S. Departments of State and Commerce

_____Canadian Department of Industry, Trade and Commerce

_____Conferences and Seminars

_____Company executives in Asia

_____Others (specify)_____

6. What <u>types</u> <u>of</u> <u>information</u> would your company <u>like</u> <u>to</u> <u>have</u> in order
   to better assess the markets of Mainland China? Please rank 1, 2,
   3 etc. in order of importance.

   _____Demand estimates of specific products/services

   _____How to negotiate with Mainland Chinese organizations

   _____Terms and conditions of financing sought by Mainland Chinese

   _____Nature of U.S. government regulations

   _____How to initiate contacts with Mainland Chinese officials

   _____Others (specify)_____

                                  IV

7. What is likely to be the <u>market</u> <u>potential</u> for your company's products
   and services in Mainland China <u>at</u> <u>present</u> and in <u>five</u> <u>years</u>? Please
   check.

	At present	In five years
High	_____	_____
Medium	_____	_____
Low	_____	_____
No demand	_____	_____

8. Which of the following <u>considerations</u> are likely to <u>influence</u> the
   <u>extent</u> <u>of</u> <u>trade</u> between the U.S.A. and Mainland China <u>at</u> <u>present</u> and
   <u>in</u> <u>five</u> <u>years</u>? Please rank 1, 2, 3 etc. in order of importance.

	At present	In five years
Growing emphasis by Mainland Chinese leaders on faster economic growth	_____	_____
Continuity of moderate, internationally oriented leadership in Mainland China	_____	_____
Mainland China's ability to export products to U.S.A. on an internationally competitive basis	_____	_____
U.S. government withdrawal of support for existing government in Taiwan	_____	_____

196

Further relaxation of U.S. restrictions
    on trade with Mainland China   _____   _____

Availability of medium-and long-term
    credit   _____   _____

Aggressive selling by U.S. companies   _____   _____

V

9. What sources is your company likely to use <u>at present</u> and <u>in five years</u> in penetrating Mainland China's markets. Please rank <u>1</u>, <u>2</u>, <u>3</u> etc. in order of importance.

	At present	In five years
Directly by U.S. parent company	_____	_____
Through an Asian affiliate (except Japan)	_____	_____
Through a Japanese affiliate	_____	_____
Through a European affiliate	_____	_____
Through a Canadian affiliate	_____	_____
Through the overseas Chinese community	_____	_____
Through established private trading companies	_____	_____
Others (specify)	_____	_____

10. What are likely to be your company's <u>key objectives at present</u> and <u>in five years</u> in penetrating Mainland China's markets? Please rank <u>1</u>, <u>2</u>, <u>3</u> etc. in order of importance.

	At present	In five years
Promote export of U.S. materials and semi-finished goods	_____	_____
Promote export of U.S. machinery and equipment	_____	_____
Obtain raw materials	_____	_____
Export to third-country markets	_____	_____

Sell technology   _____   _____

Others (specify)   _____   _____

11. What are likely to be the methods used by your company at present and in five years in penetrating Mainland China's markets? Please rank 1, 2, 3 etc. in order of importance.

	At present	In five years
Largely through exports	_____	_____
Largely through licensing	_____	_____
Largely through turnkey projects	_____	_____
Largely through production sharing arrangements	_____	_____

12. Please rank the following countries (1, 2, 3 etc.) in order of their importance as your competitors for Mainland China's markets at present and in five years.

	At present	In five years
Japan	_____	_____
West Germany	_____	_____
France	_____	_____
Italy	_____	_____
United Kingdom	_____	_____
Others (specify)	_____	_____

Thank you very much for your cooperation. We will gladly send you a copy of the results. Please indicate to whom they should be sent.

Name _____

Title _____

Address _____

                _____